KAZAKHSTAN
in Pictures

Bella Waters

TF
CB
Twenty-First Century Books

Contents

Twenty-First Century Books
A division of Lerner Publishing Group
241 First Avenue North
Minneapolis, MN 55401 U.S.A.

Website address: www.lernerbooks.com

web enhanced @ w w w . v g s b o o k s . c o m

CULTURAL LIFE   44

► Religion. Language and Literature. Art and
Architecture. Music and Dance. Food. Holidays.
Sports.

THE ECONOMY   56

► A New System. The Rich Grow Richer. Energy and
Mining. Other Industry. Agriculture. Imports and
Exports. Tourism. Transportation.
Communications. The Darker Side. The Future.

FOR MORE INFORMATION

Library of Congress Cataloging-in-Publication Data

Waters, Bella.
    Kazakhstan in pictures / by Bella Waters.
        p.   cm. — (Visual geography series)
    Includes bibliographical references and index.
    ISBN-13: 978-0-8225-6588-8 (lib. bdg. : alk. paper)
    ISBN-10: 0-8225-6588-9 (lib. bdg. : alk. paper)
    1. Kazakhstan—Pictorial works—Juvenile literature. I. Title. II. Series: Visual geography series
(Minneapolis, Minn.)
DK903.2.W38 2007
958.43—dc22   2006016522

Manufactured in the United States of America
1 2 3 4 5 6 – BP – 12 11 10 09 08 07

INTRODUCTION

Kazakhstan is a large country in central Asia. Kazakhstan has a varied and dramatic landscape, with towering mountains, rugged deserts, and vast grassy plains. It is blessed with valuable natural resources, including gold, oil, coal, and natural gas. The nation is home to about 15 million people, with a rich heritage and culture.

Kazakhstan has a long and fascinating history. Thousands of years ago, prehistoric peoples made their homes in Kazakhstan. Ancient Kazakhs were the first people in the world to tame and ride horses. The Scythian culture developed in Kazakhstan in the 600s B.C. This ancient group left behind beautiful artwork, much of it made of gold.

Through the following centuries, various outsiders invaded Kazakhstan. The newcomers brought new religions, including Islam, to Kazakhstan. Genghis Khan, a fierce warrior from Mongolia, conquered Kazakhstan in the early A.D. 1200s. His descendants ruled Kazakhstan for several centuries. In the 1500s, the Kazakhs took power for themselves. Most Kazakhs were nomads. They did not have settled homes but instead traveled from place to place with their herds of animals.

In the 1700s, Russia took control in Kazakhstan. Thousands of Russian soldiers and settlers poured into the cities and countryside. The Russian newcomers pushed the Kazakh nomads off their traditional lands. Kazakhs became second-class citizens in their own homeland.

In 1917, revolutionaries took over the Russian government. They created a new nation, the Union of Soviet Socialist Republics (USSR). Kazakhstan was one of fifteen republics in this vast new country. Under the Communist system, the Soviet government controlled every aspect of the nation's economy. The government opened new mines, farms, and factories in Kazakhstan. It told people where to work and where to live.

Under Communism, people in Kazakhstan and other Soviet republics suffered greatly. The government-run economy did not suc-ceed. People grew poor and hungry. The government also treated people

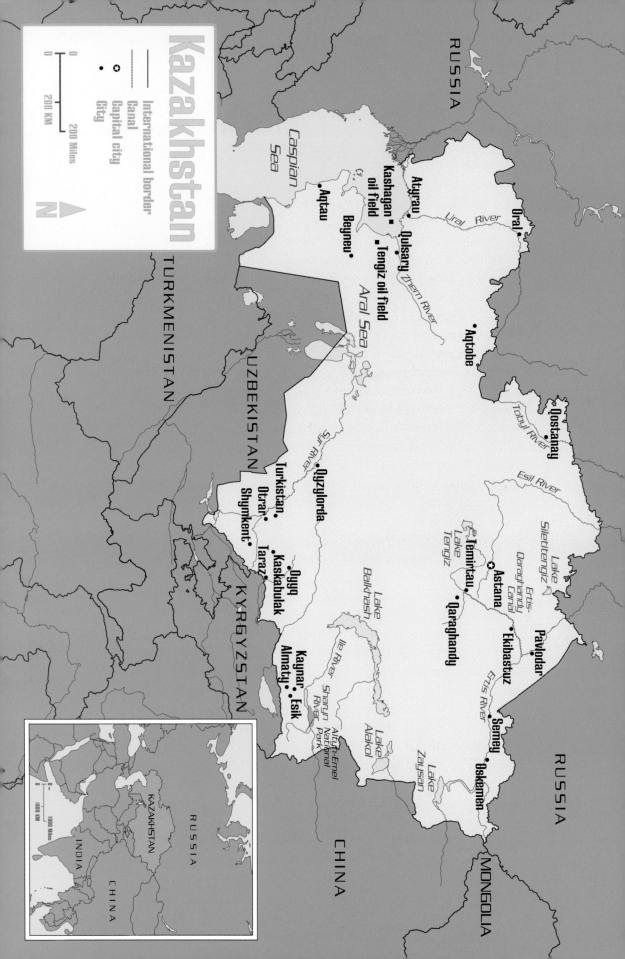

Kazakhstan

International border
Canal
Capital city
City

200 KM
200 Miles

N

RUSSIA

Caspian Sea

Aqtau

Beyneu

Kashagan oil field

Tengiz oil field

Atyrau

Qulsary

Ural River

Oral

Zhem River

Aqtobe

Aral Sea

Qostanay

Tobyl River

Esil River

Syr River

Turkistan

Otrar

Shymkent

Qyzylorda

Taraz

Oyyq

Kaskabulak

Silettengiz

Lake Tengiz

Temirtau

Astana

Ertis-Qaraghandy Canal

Qaraghandy

Ekibastuz

Pavlodar

Lake Balkhash

Kaynar

Almaty

Esik

Ile River

Sharyn River

Altyn-Emel National Park

Lake Alakol

Lake Zaysan

Ertis River

Semey

Öskemen

TURKMENISTAN

UZBEKISTAN

KYRGYZSTAN

CHINA

MONGOLIA

RUSSIA

RUSSIA

KAZAKHSTAN

INDIA

CHINA

1000 Miles
1000 KM

harshly. It denied them basic rights and freedoms, such as freedom of speech and freedom of religion. The government arrested and even killed people who opposed its policies. In Kazakhstan the Soviet government ran programs, such as the testing of deadly nuclear bombs, that hurt people and the environment.

After many years of hardship and repressive government, people in the Soviet Union began to demand change. Finally, in 1991, the Soviet Union broke apart. The Soviet republics each declared independence. Kazakhstan became an independent nation on December 16, 1991.

The new Republic of Kazakhstan switched from Communism to capitalism—an economic system based on private property and free enterprise. After a few rough years, the economy grew quickly. The oil and gas business was especially successful.

Kazakhstan also became a democratic nation. A new constitution allowed citizens to elect their own political leaders. The people of Kazakhstan enjoyed freedom of speech, freedom of the press, and other basic rights. However, Kazakhstan's first president, Nursultan Nazarbayev, did not respect these rights and freedoms. By the early 2000s, he had gathered more and more power into his own hands. Critics charged that Nazarbayev's government was corrupt, with top officials taking bribes and committing crimes.

Despite its challenges, modern Kazakhstan is a strong nation. It has a lively arts scene, a well-educated workforce, and a new capital at Astana. It is home to a mix of ethnic groups, mostly Kazakhs and Russians. Its citizens are working together to strengthen their economy, improve their environment, and protect their fragile democracy from corrupt leaders.

THE LAND

The Republic of Kazakhstan covers 1,048,300 square miles (2,715,097 square kilometers) in central Asia. The country stretches 1,056 miles (1,700 km) from north to south and 1,864 miles (3,000 km) from east to west. Kazakhstan is the ninth-largest country in the world and the second-largest country in Asia. (China is the largest.) It is almost twice as big as the U.S. state of Alaska.

Kazakhstan has no border on an ocean, but it touches two large bodies of water, the Caspian Sea to the southwest and the Aral Sea in the south. To the north, Kazakhstan shares a long border with Russia. Lying south of Kazakhstan are the central Asian republics of Turkmenistan, Uzbekistan, and Kyrgyzstan. To the east is China.

◐ Regions

Kazakhstan has five main regions. In the west is the Caspian Depression, an area of low-lying plains around the Caspian Sea. The Ustyurt Plateau, a dry, elevated region between the Caspian and Aral seas, crosses Kazakhstan's border with western Uzbekistan. The south of Kazakhstan features the Desert Region. The Greater Barsuki Desert sits northwest of the Aral Sea, while the Moyynqum and Betpaqdala deserts are found farther east. The Kyzyl Kum Desert crosses the southern border with Uzbekistan. North central Kazakhstan is covered with grassy plains called the Steppes Region. This land is good for grazing livestock. Northeastern Kazakhstan is hilly, with good farmland.

In eastern Kazakhstan is the Mountain Region. The largest peaks are the Altay (Golden) Mountains in the east and the Tian Mountains in the southeast. Mount Khan Tengri, which straddles the border between Kazakhstan and Kyrgyzstan in the Tian Mountains, is Kazakhstan's highest point. It rises 20,990 feet (6,398 meters) above sea level. Hundreds of glaciers—or slow-moving ice sheets—are found in the Tian Mountains. Smaller mountain ranges include the Qaratau Range in southern Kazakhstan and the Chu-Ily Mountains west of the city of Almaty.

Rivers and Lakes

More than seven thousand rivers flow through Kazakhstan, although many are small and dry up when they reach the nation's deserts. But a number of major rivers flow to large bodies of water. In the west, the Ural and Zhem rivers flow south from the Ural Mountains in Russia, across the Caspian Depression, and into the Caspian Sea. In the south, the Syr River begins in the Tian Mountains and eventually reaches the Aral Sea. The Ile River flows west from the Tian Mountains and empties into Lake Balkhash. The Ertis, Esil, and Tobyl rivers flow through northern Kazakhstan, cross into Russia, and eventually reach the Arctic Ocean to the north.

Kazakhstan has nearly fifty thousand lakes, most of which are less than 1 square mile (2.59 sq. km) in size. But the nation also contains several large lakes. Lake Balkhash is a long, narrow lake located in the southeastern part of the country. At 6,670 square miles (17,275 sq. km), it is the largest lake contained entirely within Kazakhstan. Other large lakes in Kazakhstan include Lake Zaysan and Lake Alakol in the east, Lake Siletitengiz in the north, and Lake Tengiz in the center of the country.

The Caspian Sea is a vast salt lake that crosses the Kazakhstani border on the west. The sea also borders Turkmenistan, Iran, Azerbaijan, and Russia. At 143,250 square miles (371,000 sq. km), the Caspian Sea is the largest inland body of water in the world. It is rich in sturgeon, a fish prized for its eggs (which are made into a delicacy called caviar). Oil and natural gas deposits are located beneath the seafloor.

The Aral Sea is another large saltwater lake. It lies in both Kazakhstan and Uzbekistan. The Aral Sea was once the fourth-largest lake in the world, measuring 25,830 square miles (66,900 sq. km) in area. But in the early 1960s, Soviet engineers began to divert water from the Syr River and the Amu River (on the Uzbekistan–Turkmenistan border), which normally flow into the sea. The engineers channeled the water to nearby cotton fields to increase central Asian cotton production. Without river water to feed it, the Aral Sea began to evaporate, or dry up.

ANOTHER SHRINKING SEA

Like the Aral Sea, Lake Balkhash in eastern Kazakhstan is shrinking. Most of the rivers that feed the lake originate in China. In recent years, the Chinese have diverted water from these rivers for farming in their own nation. As a result, Lake Balkhash has begun to dry up. Visit www.vgsbooks.com for links to websites with additional information about the evaporation of the Aral Sea and see the drastic changes that have occurred in the last fifty years.

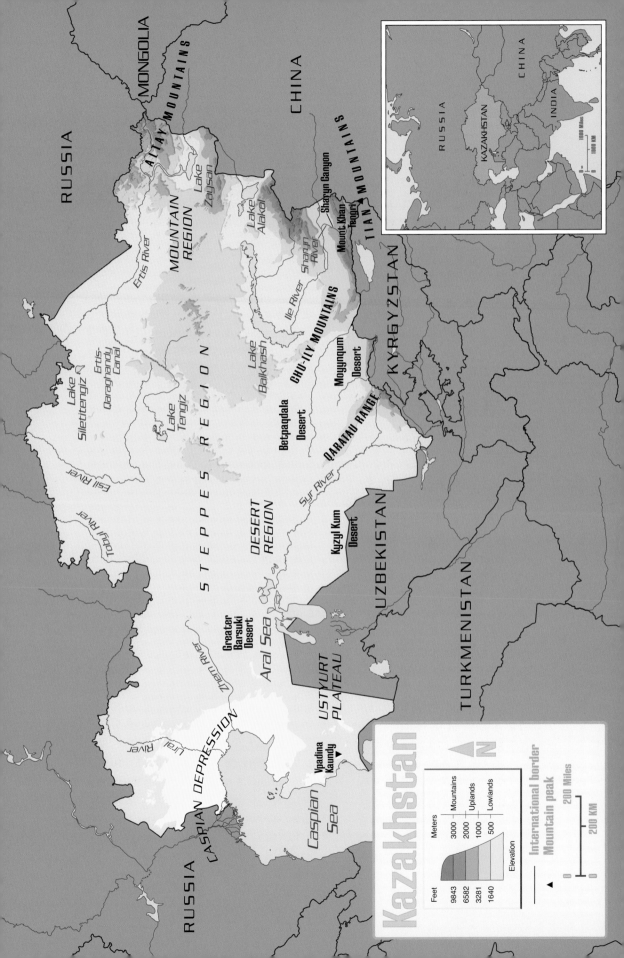

Kazakhstan

RUSSIA

MONGOLIA

CHINA

ALTAY MOUNTAINS

Lake Zaysan

Lake Alakol

MOUNTAIN REGION

Ertis River

Ertis-Qaraghandy Canal

Lake Siletitengiz

Lake Tengiz

Lake Balkhash

Ile River

Sharyn River

Sharyn Canyon

Mount Khan Tengri

TIAN MOUNTAINS

CHU-ILY MOUNTAINS

Moyynqum Desert

KYRGYZSTAN

S T E P P E S   R E G I O N

Betpaqdala Desert

QARATAU RANGE

DESERT REGION

Syr River

Kyzyl Kum Desert

UZBEKISTAN

Esil River

Tobyl River

Greater Barsuki Desert

Zhem River

Aral Sea

USTYURT PLATEAU

TURKMENISTAN

Ural River

CASPIAN DEPRESSION

Vpadina Kaundy ▲

Caspian Sea

RUSSIA

RUSSIA

CHINA

KAZAKHSTAN

INDIA

1000 Miles

1000 KM

N

200 Miles

200 KM

Feet | Meters

9843 — 3000 — Mountains
6582 — 2000 — Uplands
3281 — 1000 — Lowlands
1640 — 500

Elevation

International border
Mountain peak ▲

Two **Bactrian camels** walk past a rusty ship on a grassy plain in what used to be the Aral Sea.

By 1987 vast portions of the seabed had been exposed, and the sea had split into two sections. By the early years of the 2000s, the sea was about 40 percent of its former size.

Climate

Kazakhstan's climate varies widely. In general, the north is colder than the south, and mountains are colder than lowlands. In the northern hills, temperatures can drop as low as –40°F (–40°C) in winter. In the deserts, summer temperatures can soar as high as 113°F (45°C).

In the southern city of Almaty, the average temperature in January, the coldest month, is 16°F (–9°C). In July, the warmest month, the average temperature in Almaty is 73°F (23°C). Astana, the nation's capital, is much colder. Winter temperatures there sometimes fall below –30°F (–34°C). Blizzards often sweep through Astana and the surrounding northern steppes. The coldest parts of Kazakhstan have permafrost, or permanently frozen ground.

Most of Kazakhstan receives little precipitation (rain and snow). The desert regions of the south average about 4 inches (10 centimeters) of precipitation every year. The northern steppes get about 10 inches (25 cm). The mountains of the southeast receive about 21 inches (53 cm) of rain and snow per year. Kazakhstan is wettest in spring, when rain falls and snows melt in the mountains. Late summer and autumn can be bone dry.

◐ Flora and Fauna

Kazahkstan's plant life is as varied as its landscape. The deserts and steppes are home to small trees called saxauls, as well as sagebrush and acacia trees. Tall grasses grow on the steppes, as do abundant wildflowers, including irises, tulips, poppies, carnations, and roses. The mountains around Almaty contain cedar, larch, and fir trees, as well as wildflowers such as peonies. The nation's far north features pine and birch forests, while the south holds willows and poplars. Fruit trees, including a wide range of wild apples, grow in the southeast. Mulberries, figs, apricots, and walnuts grow there too.

Animal life also varies by location. The steppes provide a habitat for foxes, gazelles, antelope, wild sheep, wolves, and long-legged cats called caracals. Bears, ibexes, wolverines, elk, and snow leopards live in the mountains. Desert wildlife includes Bactrian camels, toads, tortoises, lizards, and snakes. Birds such as larks, ravens, warblers, sparrows, eagles, falcons, and vultures live in both the deserts and the steppes. Ducks, geese, swans, cranes, and pelicans visit northern

THE FIRST APPLES

Scientists believe that the first apple trees grew around Almaty as far back as 20 million years ago. Eventually, animals, the wind, and human travelers carried apple seeds to other places. In this way, wild apple trees spread around the world.

A street vendor sells **apples** in Almaty.

Two men use nets to fish for sturgeon in the Ural River in western Kazakhstan.

Kazakhstan in spring. Kazakhstan's rivers hold a variety of fish. The Ural and Syr rivers are famed for their sturgeon. Caspian seals live in the Caspian Sea, as do sturgeon.

Natural Resources

The list of minerals in Kazakhstan is long. In fact, almost every mineral on the periodic table of elements can be found in Kazakhstan. The list includes gold, silver, lead, zinc, copper, uranium, coal, iron ore, bauxite, molybdenum, tungsten, beryllium, titanium, and cadmium. Kazakhstan has one-third of the world's chromium and manganese and one-quarter of the world's uranium. Around and beneath the Caspian Sea are vast deposits of oil and natural gas.

Environmental Issues

Human beings have greatly impacted Kazakhstan's land and wildlife. The nation suffers from many serious environmental challenges. Perhaps the worst environmental disaster in Kazakhstan was nuclear weapons testing. Between 1949 and 1991, the Soviet government tested hundreds of nuclear bombs at six sites in Kazakhstan. Most testing took place in an area called the Semipalatinsk Polygon, near the city of Semey, in northern Kazakhstan. The nuclear fallout (radioactive particles spread by the explosions) contaminated more than 115,000 square miles (298,000 sq. km) of countryside. Because of the explosions, thousands of people living in the area grew sick with cancer and other illnesses. Many children in the region were born with birth defects.

In 1989 people in Kazakhstan organized the Nevada-Semey Movement, calling for an end to nuclear testing in Kazakhstan. In response to the group's protests, the Kazakhstani government stopped testing in 1992. Despite cleanup efforts, radiation remains in the water and soil around the Polygon. People living nearby continue to suffer from health problems.

Another environmental issue facing Kazakhstan is the destruction of the Aral Sea. The sea once had clean water, sandy beaches, many fish, and a large fishing industry. But in the 1960s, with the diversion of river water to irrigate cotton fields, the sea started to dry up. As the sea shrank, most of its fish died. Fishers could no longer make a living from the sea. Making matters worse, pesticides and fertilizers from surrounding agriculture fields polluted the remaining water. Many people who lived near the sea grew sick from water pollution. To combat the destruction, in 1992 people in central Asia founded the International Fund for Saving the Aral Sea.

The Caspian Sea also suffers from environmental problems. Industries located along the seashore, especially oil and gas facilities, have polluted the water and the land around the sea. This pollution endangers the health of people, plants, and animals.

Yet another environmental concern involves the steppes of northern Kazakhstan. These lands were once thick with grasses. For centuries, nomadic herders grazed their animals there. But starting in the 1950s, the Soviet government attempted to increase food production by turning the steppes into farmland. As part of this "Virgin (untouched) Lands Campaign," farmworkers plowed up the land and tried to grow wheat and other crops. But the farms were not successful. The soil became dry and dusty. It blew away in the wind. In many places, the once-thriving steppes turned into deserts.

Visit www.vgsbooks.com for links to websites with additional information about the Virgin Lands Campaign to bring agriculture to Kazakhstan's steppes. Find out why soil erosion happens and what can be done to prevent it.

A KAZAKHSTANI CAT

Snow leopards such as the one above live in the mountains of eastern Kazakhstan. These shy and hard-to-find animals have gray fur and black spots and may grow to weigh 150 pounds (68 kilograms). Kazakhstanis have long revered the snow leopard for its bravery, independence, and intelligence. In fact, the snow leopard is considered a national symbol in Kazakhstan.

Poaching, or illegal hunting, poses a danger to Kazakhstan's wildlife. Hunters kill snow leopards for their beautiful spotted furs. They kill saiga antelope for their horns, which are valued in China as medicine. They hunt musk deer for their musk, a substance used to make perfume. Because of illegal hunting, many animals in Kazakhstan are endangered—at risk of dying out altogether. Sturgeon and Caspian seals have been hurt by both water pollution and overhunting.

To protect wildlife, the Kazakhstani government has established a number of nature preserves and national parks, such as Ile-Alatao National Park and Bayan-Aul National Park. These lands are off-limits to hunting and other human activity. The government has also passed strict laws about hunting elsewhere. But it is not always easy to catch poachers, especially on the vast Kazakhstani steppes.

◉ Cities

Kazakhstan had few large cities before the twentieth century. Most people lived in movable tents called yurts or in small farming or trading villages. Russian settlements grew in the nineteenth century.

During World War II (1939–1945), the Soviet government opened many new factories in Kazakhstan, and cities grew larger. Growth of cities continued for the rest of the twentieth century. In the early 2000s, about 56 percent of Kazakhstanis live in urban areas.

ALMATY, Kazakhstan's former capital, has a population of 1.2 million. The city occupies a fertile area at the foot of the Tian Mountains. Almaty started out as a Russian fortress, built in 1854. Its original name was Verny, which means "loyal" in Russian. The city is prone to earthquakes. Quakes in 1887 and 1910 killed thousands of city residents.

In 1921 a political leader renamed the city Alma-Ata, which means "father of apples" in Russian. The new name referred to the many apple orchards nearby. In 1929 Alma-Ata became the capital of Soviet Kazakhstan. In 1993 the city's name was changed again. The new name was Almaty, a Kazakh-language version of Alma-Ata.

The Tian Mountains rise near the city of **Almaty.**

Modern Almaty is the largest and busiest city in Kazakhstan. It is home to museums, libraries, universities, theaters, sports arenas, grand mosques (Islamic houses of worship), and large Russian Orthodox churches. It is also the financial capital of Kazakhstan—many banks and businesses are headquartered there. In spring and summer, Almaty is an extremely green city, with trees lining almost every street.

ASTANA is a city of 500,000 people. It is located on the Esil River in northern Kazakhstan. Since 1997 Astana has been the nation's capital.

Astana traces its history to 1830, when it was founded as a Russian fortress. Its original name was Akmola, which means "white tomb." In the 1950s, the city became the hub of the Virgin Lands Campaign. The Soviet government renamed it Tselinograd, which means "Virgin Lands City." The city reclaimed the name *Akmola* after the breakup of the Soviet Union in 1991.

In 1995 President Nursultan Nazarbayev announced that he was moving the nation's capital from Almaty to Akmola, a move that took place in 1997. Not wanting a capital named White Tomb, the president renamed the city Astana, which means "capital" in Kazakh. Since becoming the capital, Astana has undergone tremendous growth. It is home to futuristic-looking government buildings, hotels, and skyscrapers. In addition to serving as government headquarters, Astana is a center for industry and food processing. It is also home to a national museum, library, and sports stadium.

QARAGHANDY is located in the heart of the Kazakhstani steppes. It is home to about 500,000 people. The region around Qaraghandy is rich in coal. The city was set up in 1856 as a coal-mining center. During the Soviet era, the government sent thousands of Russians, Germans, and Ukrainians to Qaraghandy and

The Baiterek Monument *(left)* and Tower of the Ministry *(right)* stand tall above the **Astana skyline.** New skyscrapers and high-rises are being built every day in the new capital of Kazakhstan.

nearby towns to work as coal miners, technicians, and engineers. Qaraghandy was also the site of brutal Soviet-era gulags, or prison camps. Inmates at the camps worked as slave labor in the nearby coal mines. Modern Qaraghandy is still a coal-mining town. Many residents are descendants of coal miners or prison inmates sent there in the mid-twentieth century.

The dividing line between Europe and Asia runs through Kazakhstan. At the town of Oral in northwestern Kazakhstan, a canopy marks the meeting of the two continents. Tourists like to pose for pictures there.

TARAZ, with a population of 315,000, sits on Kazakhstan's southern border with Kyrgystan. It is one of the oldest cities in Kazakhstan, with a history dating to the first century B.C. In the early centuries A.D., Taraz was a stop on the Silk Road, a series of trade routes that ran from China through central Asia to the Middle East and Europe. As a Silk Road city, Taraz received

goods, travelers, and ideas from many far-off lands. In the 1200s, Genghis Khan and his armies swept through Taraz and completely destroyed the city. Eventually, Taraz came back to life. When the Soviets took over Kazakhstan, they built many factories in Taraz. Modern Taraz is still an industrial center. It also holds two historic mausoleums (aboveground tombs), one dating to the eleventh century and the other dating to the thirteenth century.

ATYRAU, a city of 210,000, sits on the Ural River and on the north shore of the Caspian Sea. Like many big cities in Kazakhstan, it was founded as a Russian military outpost. In the past, many residents made their living by fishing in the Caspian Sea. In modern times, Atyrau has earned the nickname Oil City Kazakhstan because it sits near vast oil deposits. Gas fields also lie near the city. Giant international energy companies have built offices and facilities in Atyrau, and many city residents work in the energy industry. Atyrau is also home to mosques, museums, and Russian Orthodox churches.

HISTORY AND GOVERNMENT

People have lived in the area that would become Kazakhstan for thousands of years. In fact, archaeologists (scientists who study past human life) have found evidence of *Homo erectus*—ancestors of modern human beings—living in Kazakhstan more than two hundred thousand years ago.

Homo sapiens—modern humans—first lived in Kazakhstan about fifteen thousand years ago. Scientists have found their stone tools, pottery, cave paintings, and rock carvings at several sites. About ten thousand years ago, people in Kazakhstan became the first people in the world to tame, train, and ride horses. Soon after, they began making tools and weapons out of bronze.

An ancient group called the Scythians emerged in Kazakhstan in the 600s B.C. The Scythians kept herds of sheep, goats, cattle, horses, and camels, which provided them with meat, milk, wool, leather, and transportation. While some Scythians lived on farms and grew crops, most were nomadic—they traveled from place to place, searching for fresh grazing land for their animals. Because of their skill on horseback, the Scythians were accomplished warriors. They fought with iron weapons and occasionally battled with Persian and Greek armies. They loved gold, which they fashioned into jewelry, figurines, and other items.

Waves of Invaders

Starting in the second century B.C., various outsiders invaded and ruled Kazakhstan. First, the Usuns arrived from Mongolia in the east. In the A.D. 400s, warriors called Huns swept in from the east and north, taking power from the Usuns. The Huns ruled until the 500s, when Turkic tribes invaded from Mongolia.

Under Turkic rulers, people in Kazakhstan practiced many different religions. In the tenth century, the Karakhanid Turks took over Kazakhstan. Karakhanid leaders practiced Islam, a religion that had been founded in Arabia in the seventh century. The Karakhanid Turks spread Islam throughout much of Kazakhstan.

The next rulers of Kazakhstan were the Khitans, who invaded from northern China in 1130. Khitan rule lasted less than a century. In the early 1200s, a warrior called Genghis Khan (which means "most mighty prince") came to power in Mongolia. He united several Mongol tribes under his command. In the 1220s, his armies conquered central Asia.

Genghis Khan

Genghis Khan died in 1227, and his empire was split into three regions, known as hordes, each controlled by one of his sons. Western and northern Kazakhstan belonged to the Golden Horde. The rest of Kazakhstan was part of the Blue Horde. (The third horde encompassed China and Mongolia.) Berke Khan, Genghis Khan's grandson, took over the Golden Horde in 1258. Berke practiced the Islamic faith and made Islam the official religion of his territory.

After suffering several defeats, the Mongol Empire began to weaken in the fourteenth century. Seeking to revive the great empire, a warrior named Timur (also descended from Genghis Khan) amassed a huge army. With his capital at Samarqand in modern-day Uzbekistan, Timur conquered much of central Asia and the Middle East. A devout Muslim (a member of the Islamic faith), Timur oversaw the building of great mosques throughout his empire.

The Kazakhs

After Timur's death in 1405, his empire broke apart. Central Asia split into several khanates (regions under the rule of a khan, or prince). The strongest of these were the Nogai Khanate and the Uzbek Khanate. In the 1500s, a number of clans (groups of families) broke away from the Uzbek Khanate and moved into the river valleys around Lake Balkhash. These clans took the name *Kazakhs*, which means "adventurer" or "outlaw." Unlike the Uzbeks, who lived a settled lifestyle, the Kazakhs were nomads.

Under their leader, Kasym Khan, the Kazakhs expanded across much of the territory of modern Kazakhstan. Within this area, three new hordes emerged—the Great Horde of southeastern Kazakhstan, the Middle Horde in the center and northeast, and the Little Horde in the west.

The Kazakh hordes frequently warred among themselves. They also fought enemies who lived along their borders. One of their strongest foes was the Russian Empire, located to the west and north. The Russians often clashed with the Kazakhs of the Little Horde.

Another Kazakh enemy was the Jungars, a warlike nomadic group from western China. In the late seventeenth and early eighteenth centuries, the Jungars made bloody raids into Kazakh territory. Fearful of the Jungars, in the early 1700s, the Kazakhs decided to make a deal with their old enemies the Russians. One by one, the leaders of the three hordes asked Russia for protection from the Jungar threat. In exchange for this protection, the Kazakh hordes swore loyalty to the Russian czar, or emperor.

The Russians Are Coming

The Kazakhs and the Russians had different views on what "Russian protection" and "loyalty to the czar" involved. The Kazakhs believed they had simply made a political and military alliance with the Russians but would retain their independence. The Russians saw the situation differently. They believed the agreements with the hordes entitled them to annex, or take over, Kazakh territory.

Russia quickly set about taking power in Kazakhstan. In the mid-1700s, it sent thousands of soldiers and settlers to live in Kazakhstan. The newcomers built forts, farms, and cities across the steppes. They declared that Kazakh nomads could not travel freely across the land with their animals.

In the 1700s, the Kazakhs started to rebel against Russian rule. Kazakh fighters attacked Russian forts and settlements. But Russian military power was too strong. Throughout the nineteenth century, Russian soldiers put down a number of Kazakh revolts.

THE GOLDEN MAN

In 1969, in the town of Esik near Almaty, archaeologists found the grave of a Scythian warrior. The grave contained a fabulous costume *(below)*, including boots, belts, armor, and an elaborate headdress. The outfit was made from red cloth and decorated with four thousand pieces of gold from head to toe—leading to the name Golden Man for the warrior who once wore it.

More and more Russian settlers poured into Kazakhstan. As they did, society became divided. On one side were the nomadic Kazakhs, who mostly practiced the Islamic faith. On the other side were the Russians. They lived settled lives on farms and in cities. They mostly practiced the Russian Orthodox faith, a form of Christianity.

The Russian government put Russians in charge of Kazakhstan. Native Kazakhs became second-class citizens in their own territory. Russia taxed them heavily and continued to restrict their travel across the steppes. Without adequate grazing land for their animals, the nomadic Kazakhs could not survive. Some began to starve. And the Russians kept coming. By the early 1900s, Russians made up more than 40 percent of the Kazakhstani population.

In 1914 Russia entered World War I (1914–1918). To feed, clothe, and equip its armies, Russia needed meat, animal hides, and horses. It seized hundreds of thousands of animals from Kazakh herders, who received no payment in return. The Russian government also called up tens of thousands of Kazakh men to serve as military laborers. The Kazakhs wanted no part in the Russian war effort. By 1916 they had organized another resistance movement. In numerous cities, thousands of Kazakh fighters clashed with Russian troops. But again the Russians proved too powerful. The 1916 uprising failed.

Visit www.vgsbooks.com for links to websites with additional information about the impact of the Russian Revolution and the Cold War in Kazakhstan.

Communists in Charge

The year 1917 was one of dramatic change in Russia. That year political revolutionaries called Bolsheviks seized control of the Russian government in an event called the Russian Revolution. The Bolsheviks set up a new political and economic system throughout the Russian Empire. Under this system, called Communism, the central government completely controlled the nation's business and economy.

The Bolshevik takeover led to a civil war. Communist (Red Army) and non-Communist (White Army) forces battled one another for control of Russian territory. Seeing an opportunity to gain self-rule during this conflict, Kazakhs organized under the banner of the Alash Orda Party, which sided with the White Army against the communists. More than one million Kazakhs died during the fighting. The Red

Army finally defeated the Alash Orda and other White forces in the early 1920s.

With their power solidified, in 1922 the Communists created a new nation, the Union of Soviet Socialist Republics (the Soviet Union). The Soviet Union was made up of fifteen republics, including Kazakhstan. (The republic had three different names during the Soviet era: first, it was called the Kyrgyz Autonomous Soviet Socialist Republic, then the Kazakh Autonomous Soviet Socialist Republic, and finally the Kazakh Soviet Socialist Republic.) Communist leaders controlled the nation from Moscow, Russia, the Soviet capital. They appointed Communist officials to govern in each republic.

The Soviet government ruled with an iron hand. It denied people freedom of speech, freedom of the press, fair trials, the right to vote, and other basic rights. Even religion was forbidden. The government told people where to work, where to live, and even what to think. There was only one legal political party—the Communist Party. Anyone who spoke out against the party or the Communist system risked arrest or even execution.

Joseph Stalin, who came to power in the Soviet Union in 1929, was a particularly brutal dictator. Using a secret police force, he arrested and killed anyone seen as a threat to his power—even loyal Communist Party members. Stalin set up gulags throughout the Soviet Union. Because Kazakhstan was cold, vast, and far from big Soviet cities, Stalin located many gulags there. Millions of prisoners died in the camps.

In keeping with Communist philosophy, the government controlled the economy of the Soviet Union. The Soviet government opened big mines, oil wells, and factories in Kazakhstan. It also created collectives—large state-run farms. The government then forced thousands of nomadic people to give up their mobile way of life. Some became workers in government-run mines and factories. Most moved to collective farms, where they worked as farm laborers.

After the harvest each year, the government took most of the crops for distribution elsewhere in the

A DAY IN THE LIFE

Aleksandr Solzhenitsyn was a Soviet army officer who dared to criticize Joseph Stalin in a private letter to a friend. As punishment, the Soviet government sent Solzhenitsyn to a gulag near Qaraghandy. He chronicled his experiences of hunger, cold, and mistreatment in a novel, *One Day in the Life of Ivan Denisovich* (1962). With this work and others, Solzhenitsyn brought international attention to the brutal Soviet gulag system.

Soviet Union. But the farms did not produce as much crops as the government planners expected or wanted. Some Kazakhs even burned their own grain and slaughtered their own animals rather than hand them over to the government. Collective farming was a failure, and workers grew hungry and then sick. Epidemics of disease swept through Kazakhstan.

Historians estimate that from 1929 until 1939, between 1.75 and 2 million Kazakhs died of starvation, disease, or execution at the hands of Soviet authorities. More than 200,000 Kazakhs fled their homeland during this period. They moved to nearby lands, including China, Mongolia, Afghanistan, and Iran.

◗ Hot and Cold Wars

In 1938 German leader Adolf Hitler started gaining control of neighboring states in Europe. Hitler's actions led to the outbreak of World War II. Although Joseph Stalin had signed a peace treaty with Hitler, the German leader attacked the western Soviet

THE SPACE RACE

Kazakhstan is home to the Baikonur Cosmodrome, located east of the Aral Sea on the Syr River. Built in 1955, Baikonur was headquarters for the Soviet space program from the 1950s to the 1980s. Many historic flights launched from Baikonur. *Sputnik 1*, the first spacecraft to orbit Earth, took off from Baikonur in 1957. Yuri Gagarin *(below)*, the first human to travel in space, launched from Baikonur in 1961. After the breakup of the Soviet Union, the Russian Federal Space Agency took over the center, which it rents from Kazakhstan.

Union in June 1941. Thus the Soviet Union entered the war on the side of the Allies—the nations fighting Germany.

Kazakhstan played an important role during World War II. The Soviet government moved factories to Kazakhstan to keep them safe from Germany's military. To make weapons and military equipment, the government also mined and processed Kazakhstan's iron, lead, and copper. More than one million Kazakhs, including many women, served in the Soviet army during the war. The Soviet Union was made up of dozens of ethnic groups, including Germans who had moved to Soviet territory many years earlier. Joseph Stalin feared that Germans and other ethnic citizens might be loyal to the enemy. So Stalin rounded up thousands of ethnic Soviets, including Germans, Koreans, Tatars, and Chechens, and moved them to remote Kazakhstan and other central Asian republics. When the war ended with an Allied victory in 1945, most deportees remained in Kazakhstan. In most cases, the Soviet government did not permit them to return home.

The end of World War II saw the beginning of a new kind of war, called the Cold War (1945–1991), during which the Communist Soviet Union and the capitalist United States competed to become the world's most powerful nation. Each nation built up large stockpiles of nuclear and conventional weapons, although they never engaged in direct military conflict.

In 1949 the Soviet Union began to test nuclear weapons at six sites around Kazakhstan. The principal testing site was near Semipalatinsk (modern-day Semey) in northeastern Kazakhstan. To study the effects of nuclear bombs on living things, the Soviet government brought animals and people close to the test sites. Many test subjects, as well as those already living near test sites, later developed cancer and other health problems caused by nuclear fallout.

A Failing System

Life under Communism had advantages and disadvantages. On the positive side, the government gave every citizen a place to live and a job. It provided free education and health care to all citizens. But the system had many negatives. The planned economy was inefficient. Most ordinary people lived in poverty. Only top Communist Party leaders had cars or nice homes. And people suffered under harsh government repression.

In 1958 Soviet leader Nikita Khrushchev devised a plan. To help feed the Soviet people,

Nikita Khrushchev

Tractors harvest wheat on the Kazakhstani steppes during the Virgin Lands Campaign. Eventually the soil lost all its nutrients and would not produce crops.

he decided to grow wheat, corn, and other grain on the Kazakhstani steppes. As part of the plan, called the Virgin Lands Campaign, the government set up new farms across 100,000 square miles (259,000 sq. km) of north central Kazakhstan. The government sent about two million migrants from other parts of the Soviet Union to work the farms. Engineers diverted water from the Amu River south of Kazakhstan and the Syr River in southern Kazakhstan to irrigate the new farmland.

The harvests of grain were large at first, but success did not last. The soil of the steppes was not rich enough for growing crops. The region didn't receive plentiful rainfall. Although farmers continued to work the land, the Virgin Lands Campaign was a failure. Unable to grow enough grain to feed its people, the Soviet Union was forced to import grain from foreign countries.

Throughout the 1960s and 1970s, the Soviet economy continued to suffer. People faced shortages of food and consumer goods. By the 1980s, the Soviet people were fed up with Communism. They saw that people in non-Communist countries, such as the United States, had big homes, fancy cars, and plenty of food. But most of all, Soviet citizens envied the freedom that people in non-Communist countries enjoyed. Soviet citizens began to demand change.

Push for Freedom

Mikhail Gorbachev, who became the Soviet leader in 1985, saw that the Soviet system was broken. He introduced a policy called perestroika, or "restructuring." Under perestroika, the government loosened its control of the Soviet economy. For the first time, people could run their own small businesses. Perestroika also involved political reforms. For instance, people were allowed to form new, non-Communist political parties. Gorbachev introduced another policy called glasnost, or "openness." Glasnost allowed Soviet citizens to express their political views more freely. But some citizens were not content with simple reform of the Soviet system. In many republics, people pushed for complete independence from the Soviet Union.

In Kazakhstan, after centuries of immigration by Russians and other ethnic groups, Kazakhs had become a minority in their own homeland. But Kazakhs still had ethnic pride and a desire to run their own affairs. So in December 1986, when the Soviet government appointed a Russian, Gennady Kolbin, as head of the Communist Party of Kazakhstan, Kazakhs grew angry. About three thousand anti-Kolbin protesters took to the streets of Alma-Ata (modern-day Almaty). Police used force to disperse the crowds, killing several people and injuring many more.

In June 1989, Mikhail Gorbachev calmed the situation. He named Nursultan Nazarbayev, an ethnic Kazakh, to replace Kolbin. Nazarbayev favored Gorbachev's economic and political reforms. He also championed Kazakh pride. Under his leadership, Kazakh joined Russian as an official language of Kazakhstan.

But other Communist Party members opposed Gorbachev's policies. They feared that perestroika and glasnost would lead to the loss of Communist power. So on August 19, 1991, a group of military and political leaders arrested Gorbachev and attempted a coup d'état, or seizure of power. But the coup plotters failed to win the support of the Soviet people. Within a few days, the coup collapsed. Gorbachev was released, and the coup plotters were arrested.

A New Republic

The attempted coup further weakened the Soviet government. Within weeks, Soviet republics began declaring independence from the Soviet Union. Kazakhstan declared its independence on December 16, 1991. The nation's new name was the Republic of Kazakhstan.

That same month, Nursultan Nazarbayev, running without an opponent, was elected the first president of an independent Kazakhstan. Also in December, Kazakhstan joined the Commonwealth of Independent States, an association of former Soviet republics.

Nursultan Nazarbayev gradually tightened his control over all branches of the Kazakhstani government.

In March 1992, Kazakhstan joined the United Nations. In 1993 Kazakhstan signed on to an international treaty calling for the reduction and control of nuclear weapons. Under this treaty, Kazakhstan gave all its nuclear weapons to Russia.

President Nazarbayev had bold economic plans for Kazakhstan. The nation had many newly discovered oil and natural gas fields. The government signed agreements with several foreign oil companies. The companies began building pipelines and other facilities for carrying Kazakhstani oil to the world market. The Kazakhstani government also began the switch from a Communist economy to a capitalist economy. The government sold state-owned industries to private owners, distributed state land to individual farmers, and encouraged foreign companies to invest in Kazakhstan.

While President Nazarbayev made important strides for his nation's economy, he also made some troubling moves. In a series of political maneuvers in the mid-1990s, he changed Kazakhstan's constitution, extended his term in office, and gathered more power into his own hands. He also handed out important jobs to family members.

WHAT'S IN A NAME?

Stan is an ancient Persian word meaning "land" or "nation." Thus Kazakhstan is "the land of the Kazakhs," Uzbekistan is "the land of the Uzbeks," Tajikistan is "the land of the Tajiks," and so on.

People inside and outside Kazakhstan feared that Nazarbayev was starting to rule as a dictator.

In 1995 Nazarbayev surprised many when he announced that he was moving the nation's capital from Almaty in the south to Astana in the north, a move that took place in late 1997. The move baffled observers. Astana was far from other big cities and at the time was hard to reach by road or air. But Astana had many Russian inhabitants. Some experts think Nazarbayev moved the capital there to strengthen ties with Russia and to keep ethnic Russians from leaving Kazakhstan.

Kazakhstan also strengthened its ties with the Western world after the September 11, 2001, terrorist attacks on the United States. In the wake of the attacks, Kazakhstan expressed its sympathy and support for the United States. It also offered its assistance in the global war on terror. When a coalition of countries led by the United States went to

The central square of Astana, the capital of Kazakhstan since 1997. The House of Government is on the left, and the headquarters of the legislature is on the right. The goverment completed its move to Astana in 2000. New residents continue to increase the size of the once obscure city in north central Kazakhstan.

Kazakhstani soldiers march in a ceremony near the southern Iraqi city of Kut.

war with Iraq in 2003, Kazakhstan sent about thirty troops to aid the coalition.

The first decade of the 2000s showed more troubling signs in Kazakhstan. President Nazarbayev further tightened his grip on power. He had political opponents arrested and thrown in jail. Two opponents were shot dead—likely on Nazarbayev's orders. Nazarbayev also threatened journalists and shut down newspapers that criticized him. Critics charged that Nazarbayev's government was corrupt, with judges, police officers, and high government officials taking bribes and committing crimes.

In December 2005, Nazarbayev was reelected president with more than 90 percent of the vote. But human rights groups charged that the election was neither free nor fair. In January 2006, Nazarbayev began a new seven-year term.

Some international observers have denounced President Nazarbayev for abandoning democratic principles. But the United States, Russia, China, and other powerful nations are still friendly with Kazakhstan. These countries want good business relations with Kazakhstan. They want to keep buying Kazakhstani oil and natural gas and do not want to offend President Nazarbayev by criticizing his government.

Government

Kazakhstan is organized as a republic—a nation in which citizens vote for their elected leaders. All citizens aged eighteen and older are eligible to vote.

Citizens vote for a president, who serves a seven-year term with no term limits. The president appoints a Council of Ministers, including a prime minister. The ministers run various government agencies, such as the Ministry of Finance, the Ministry of Defense, and the Ministry of Health. The prime minister oversees day-to-day government operations.

Kazakhstan's legislative, or lawmaking, branch consists of two houses: a thirty-nine-member Senate and a seventy-seven-member Assembly. The president appoints seven senators; voters elect the rest. Senators serve for six-year terms. Voters elect all Assembly members, who serve five-year terms.

The nation's judicial branch consists of several layers of courts. District courts and regional courts handle most criminal and civil (noncriminal) cases. The president appoints district and regional court judges. The Supreme Court is the highest court in the land. This court has forty-four members, nominated by the president and appointed by the Senate. Kazakhstan also has special courts, such as economic courts that hear cases involving business disputes, and courts of appeal, which review lower court decisions.

For purposes of local government, Kazakhstan is divided into fourteen provinces and three cities. Each territory is headed by a governor, appointed by the president.

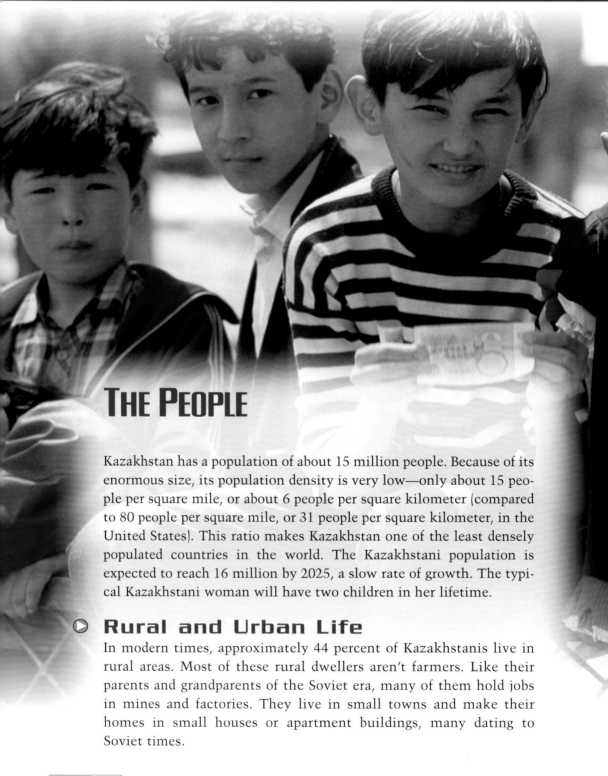

THE PEOPLE

Kazakhstan has a population of about 15 million people. Because of its enormous size, its population density is very low—only about 15 people per square mile, or about 6 people per square kilometer (compared to 80 people per square mile, or 31 people per square kilometer, in the United States). This ratio makes Kazakhstan one of the least densely populated countries in the world. The Kazakhstani population is expected to reach 16 million by 2025, a slow rate of growth. The typical Kazakhstani woman will have two children in her lifetime.

◉ Rural and Urban Life

In modern times, approximately 44 percent of Kazakhstanis live in rural areas. Most of these rural dwellers aren't farmers. Like their parents and grandparents of the Soviet era, many of them hold jobs in mines and factories. They live in small towns and make their homes in small houses or apartment buildings, many dating to Soviet times.

Some rural dwellers do farm the land. Some farmers grow crops, while others raise livestock. Most Kazakhstani farmers use modern farm vehicles, such as tractors and trucks. But a small fraction of Kazakhstanis carry on the traditions of their ancestors. Riding on horseback, they travel across the steppes with their livestock. Some even live in yurts in summer, although most also have modern-style homes.

The remaining 56 percent of Kazakhstanis are urban dwellers. They live in big cities such as Astana and Almaty. City dwellers work at many different kinds of jobs. They are teachers, government employees, factory workers, or engineers, depending on their training and the jobs available nearby. Kazakhstan's big cities look a lot like big cities in the United States, with traffic jams, big office buildings, stores, and restaurants.

Ethnic Groups

Kazakhstan's ethnic mix has fluctuated greatly in the last few centuries. Before the 1700s, the majority of people were native Kazakhs.

A nomad herds her sheep near her **yurt.** Few Kazakhs still lead a nomadic lifestyle. To learn how to build a yurt, visit www.vgsbooks.com for links.

LIVING ON THE ROAD

Kazakh nomads had no permanent homes. Instead, they lived in yurts, which were easy to construct, take down, and move from place to place. The typical yurt was made of a round wooden frame, covered by layers of felt (heavy woolen cloth). The word *yurt* comes from a Kazakh word that means "community," "people," or "family."

But in the 1700s, settlers started to arrive in Kazakhstan from Russia. By the time of the Russian Revolution, Russians made up almost half of the Kazakhstani population. The Russian newcomers dominated Kazakhstani society. They took over government and business. Russian became the nation's primary language.

Under Soviet control, the ethnic mix changed further. The government sent more Russians to farm and work in Kazakhstan. At the same time, thousands of native Kazakhs, fearful of the Soviet authorities, fled their homeland for nearby nations (these exiled Kazakhs are called Oralmans). During World War II, worried that ethnic Soviets would assist the enemy, the Soviet government sent Germans, Koreans, Chechens, Tatars, and many other ethnic peoples to live in Kazakhstan, far from the front lines. Finally, during the Virgin Lands Campaign of the 1950s and 1960s, the government sent even more non-Kazakhs to work in Kazakhstan. By the 1960s, Kazakhs comprised less than 35 percent of the Kazakhstani population. They had become a minority in their own homeland.

After the Soviet Union fell apart in the early 1990s, people in the former Soviet republics were free to live wherever they pleased. Thousands of ethnic Russians, Germans, and others living in Kazakhstan chose to return to the lands of their ancestors. At the same time, thousands of Oralmans returned to Kazakhstan. The number of Kazakhs, as a percentage of the overall population, began to grow.

By 2005 the ethnic situation had stabilized. Kazakhs made up approximately 53 percent of the population. Russians made up 30 percent. Other ethnic groups included Ukrainians (3.7 percent), Uzbeks (2.5 percent), Germans (2.4 percent), Tatars (1.7 percent), and Uygurs (1.4 percent). Various other groups, including Koreans and Kurds, make up approximately 5 percent of the population.

In modern-day Kazakhstan, most ethnic Russians, Ukrainians, and Germans tend to live in the north and west, nearest the Russian border. Ethnic Kazakhs, Uzbeks, Tatars, and Uygurs are concentrated in the south and east. Each group

TRADITIONAL CLOTHING

In earlier centuries, Kazakhstanis wore traditional dress. For example, in winter, men wore fur or leather jackets, wool or camel hair coats, thick wool-lined trousers, and high-heeled leather boots. On their heads, men wore sharply pointed hats, trimmed with the fur of foxes, sables, or minks. In summer men wore clothing made of goat or antelope hides, thin felt caps, and light boots or sandals.

Women also wore warm boots, dresses, and coats lined with animal skins and furs. Unmarried women wore cone-shaped hats trimmed with fur, feathers, or beads. Married women wore large kerchiefs wound around their heads. For special occasions, women wore dresses made of silk, cotton, or velvet, topped by a woolen vest or jacket embroidered with gold or silver thread.

In modern times, Kazakhstanis dress in traditional costumes for festivals, holidays, and other special occasions. Most of the time, however, they dress in modern-style clothing, similar to styles seen in the United States.

Ethnic Russian Kazakhstanis in costume celebrate the Russian summer solstice holiday of Ivan Kupala in the northern capital city of Astana.

carries on its own language, customs, and religious traditions. Sometimes ethnic relations are tense, especially between Kazakhs and Russians. But in general, the different groups get along peacefully.

◎ Education

Prior to the twentieth century, few Kazakhstani children attended school. Instead, they worked at home with their parents, tending livestock and performing other farm chores. A small number of boys attended religious schools, where they studied the principles of Islam. The language of instruction was Kazakh.

After Kazakhstan became part of the Soviet Union, schooling changed. The government shut down religious schools and opened secular (nonreligious) schools for Kazakhstani children. Many schools used Russian as the language of instruction, although others retained

Kazakh. Soviet-run schools trained children in academic subjects as well as the principles of Communism.

With independence, schooling changed again. Students no longer studied Communist principles in school. Religious schools—which had been banned by the Soviet government—were free to operate once more. But the Kazakhstani school system suffered in the early years of independence. The economy took a downturn, which meant there was less money for schools. Schools fell into disrepair. They faced shortages of teachers and supplies. But gradually, during the late 1990s and early 2000s, the economy picked up and the nation's school system improved.

In modern Kazakhstan, school is free and required for all children ages five to sixteen. Most school-age children attend school, although some teenagers drop out before graduation and take jobs. Kazakh and Russian are the primary languages of instruction, depending on the language of the local community. Some Kazakhstani children attend special job training schools, religious schools (both Islamic and Russian Orthodox), or schools for children with special needs.

Schoolchildren in the western city of Qulsary study their lessons.

Kazakhstan is home to more than 150 colleges and universities. There, students train for jobs in law, teaching, accounting, engineering, and other professions. Overall, Kazakhstan has a very well-educated population. The literacy rate (percentage of people who can read and write) is high—99 percent for men and 98 percent for women.

Health Issues

The Kazakhstani government provides some free health care to citizens, while private hospitals and clinics also treat many patients. However, not all Kazakhstanis have easy access to health care. Doctors and hospitals tend to be located in big cities, while many rural areas lack facilities. In addition, government spending on health care is low, leading to poor care at some government facilities. As a result, many poor Kazakhstanis don't receive high-quality health care.

National statistics reveal that Kazakhstan faces some serious health problems. The nation's infant mortality rate—the number of children who die around the time of birth—is high. The rate is 61 deaths per 1,000 births (compared to just 7 deaths per 1,000 births in the United States). Life expectancy is fair: 61 years for men and 72 years for women (compared to 75 years for men and 80 years for women in the United States).

Some health problems in Kazakhstan stem from environmental pollution. For instance, pesticides, fertilizers, and industrial waste have polluted many rivers and lakes (including the Aral Sea and the Caspian Sea). Some of this pollution contaminates drinking water supplies, leading to cancer and other diseases. Kazakhstan also suffers from air pollution, which causes lung ailments such as asthma.

Some of the worst health problems in Kazakhstan are linked to extensive nuclear weapons testing in the mid- and late twentieth century. People living around Semey and other nuclear test sites still suffer from high rates of cancer. Many children in these regions are stillborn (dead at birth). Others have severe birth defects.

A growing health problem in Kazakhstan is HIV (human immunodeficiency virus). HIV is the virus that causes AIDS (acquired immunodeficiency syndrome). Without medical treatment, AIDS is a fatal disease. HIV is transmitted by body fluids, most commonly through sexual contact or intravenous drug use.

Visit www.vgsbooks.com for links to websites with additional information about the health issues facing the Kazakhstani people.

Kazakhstanis eat a meal at a **children's leukemia center.** Cases of leukemia and other forms of cancer have risen dramatically in Kazakhstan due to environmental pollution and nuclear fallout.

The HIV rate in Kazakhstan is low—less than 0.2 percent of adults are infected with the virus. However, rates of intravenous drug use are rising in Kazakhstan, leading to rising rates of HIV infection. The Kazakhstani government is working with international groups such as the World Health Organization (WHO) to treat people with HIV/AIDS and to educate people about HIV prevention.

Women's Rights

Traditionally, Kazakh women had to be strong and hardy. As nomads, they traveled year-round. Women rode horseback, tended animals, and constructed yurts. They were also in charge of cooking and housekeeping. At the same time, however, the man was the head of the family. Women were expected to obey their husbands.

With the creation of the Soviet Union, women in Kazakhstan took on new roles. The government gave jobs to all adults—male and female. Government-run day-care programs looked after children when parents worked. The government also educated girls and boys equally. As a result, women played a sizable role in business, education, and government during the Soviet era. During World War II, many Kazakhstani women served as combat soldiers.

REAL-LIFE AMAZONS

For centuries, the ancient Greeks and Romans told stories of female warriors called Amazons. For a long time, scholars dismissed these stories as myths. But in recent years, historians have found evidence that Scythian women of the seventh to the third centuries B.C. did fight as warriors. At burial sites in Kazakhstan, archaeologists have uncovered weapons that women used in battle. They have also found headdresses, charms, and other objects indicating that Scythian women also served as priestesses.

In post-Soviet Kazakhstan, women enjoy equal rights with men. The constitution forbids discrimination on the basis of gender. Modern Kazakhstani women work and attend school alongside men. However, men generally earn more money than women, even for doing the same jobs. Men generally hold the top positions in business and government. In the early 2000s, women make up only 10 percent of Kazakhstan's legislature.

Despite having a measure of equality with men, Kazakhstani women face some troubling problems. Statistics show that more than 30 percent of women suffer from domestic violence (physical abuse at the hands of

Women in Almaty wait for a bus. **Modern Kazakhstani women** have equal legal rights with men but are not always paid as much as men for the same job.

male members of their household). Some women and girls in Kazakhstan fall victim to human traffickers. The traffickers are criminals who promise women jobs in foreign countries, then force them to work as prostitutes (sex workers). The Kazakhstani government has passed laws to combat both domestic violence and human trafficking.

Visit www.vgsbooks.com for links to websites with additional information about the people of Kazakhstan, including up-to-date demographics.

CULTURAL LIFE

Kazakhstan has a rich cultural mix. It has an Asian flavor in the east and a Russian feel in the west. It also retains many elements of its ancient cultures, including ancient religions and artistic traditions. These cultural elements combine to give Kazakhstan a vibrant arts scene.

Religion

Early peoples in Kazakhstan practiced a faith called Tengrism. Tengrists believed in the unity of heaven and earth. They saw all nature—rivers, mountains, trees, and the sky—as holy. They believed in good and evil spirits and worshipped the spirits of their ancestors. Priests performed elaborate ceremonies, asking the spirits for good fortune.

Over the centuries, various invaders brought new religions to Kazakhstan. These included Buddhism (from Asia), Zoroastrianism (from Persia, or modern-day Iran), and Judaism and Christianity (from the Middle East). Kazakhstan became religiously diverse, although Tengrism remained the dominant faith.

Starting in the tenth century, Islam began to spread through Kazakhstan. New leaders actively promoted the faith. By the fifteenth century, Islam had become the main religion in Kazakhstan. Many people practiced Sufism, a mystical branch of Islam. But people did not give up on Tengrism entirely. They combined Islamic practice with their ancient Tengrist beliefs, creating a unique hybrid religion.

In the 1700s, Russian settlers arrived in Kazakhstan. Most Russians practiced the Russian Orthodox form of Christianity. The Russians built magnificent churches in cities throughout Kazakhstan. Where the Russian population was large, Orthodox Christianity became the dominant faith.

The formation of the Soviet Union struck a blow to religion in Kazakhstan and all other Soviet republics. Soviet leaders frowned on religion. They thought it was superstition and not suitable for a modern, efficient state. The Soviet government banned religious worship throughout the Soviet Union. It destroyed churches, mosques, and

The **Central Mosque,** an Islamic house of worship, in Almaty was completed in 1999. The mosque can hold more than three thousand worshippers.

synagogues (Jewish houses of worship) and arrested religious leaders. Some Soviet people continued to practice their religion, but they had to do so in secret.

With the fall of the Soviet Union, people were free to practice religion once more. In Kazakhstan, people repaired old religious buildings. They also built new ones. In modern-day Kazakhstan, 47 percent of the population calls itself Islamic. However, only a small fraction of this group actively practices the faith. Another 44 percent identifies itself as Russian Orthodox. But again, most of these people do not regularly attend church. Protestants (mostly people of German heritage) account for 2 percent of the Kazakhstani population. The remaining 7 percent of Kazakhstanis practice another religion, such as Buddhism, Catholicism, or Judaism.

Kazakhstan has always had a small Jewish community. But after independence, many Kazakhstani Jews chose to move to Israel, the Jewish state in the Middle East.

Interestingly, many Kazakhstanis still carry on Tengrist beliefs. For instance, people often tie strips of cloth to tree branches, usually near a body of water. This ancient Tengrist practice is meant to bring people closer to heaven, spirits, and their ancestors. People also revere Mount Khan Tengri, the tallest peak in Kazakhstan and the holiest site of ancient times. It is said to be a bridge between heaven and earth.

Language and Literature

Kazakh is the native language of Kazakhstan. In earlier centuries, Kazakh was not a written language. People passed on history, religion, and culture orally—that is, by word of mouth. They listened to poets, singers, and storytellers. Epic poems (large poems originally relayed through oral tradition) told of the adventures of Kazakh warriors and heroes.

Around the 1600s, poets and storytellers began to record their works on paper. They wrote Kazakh using Arabic script, the alphabet of the Middle East. This alphabet had arrived in Kazakhstan with the Islamic religion. Abai Kananbaev (1845–1904) was the first well-known Kazakhstani poet.

Russian settlers brought the Russian language to Kazakhstan. They wrote their language using the Cyrillic alphabet. After Russians took power in Kazakhstan, Russian became the dominant language in business, government, and schools (and Cyrillic became the dominant script). Many Kazakh speakers learned Russian, although few Russians learned Kazakh. During the Soviet era, the Russian language continued to dominate. But in their homes and communities, native Kazakhs still used the Kazakh language.

The Soviet era was a difficult time for writers in Kazakhstan and other Soviet republics. Government officials reviewed all literature before publication. Works that criticized the government or the Communist system were not allowed. To keep them from stirring up anti-Communist feelings, Soviet leader Joseph Stalin had many Kazakhstani writers arrested and put to death.

Since the fall of the Soviet Union, Kazakhstani writers have more freedom to express their ideas and feelings. Some contemporary writers such as Olzhas Suleimenov have written about life since Communism. Others have explored Kazakhstan's nomadic history.

In the early 2000s, Kazakhstan remains a bilingual country. Officially, Kazakh is the state language, while Russian is the "language of interethnic communication." Many Kazakhstanis speak both languages, but Russian is more widely spoken, especially in business. Many young people also study and speak English, the language of international business.

Art and Architecture

Art in Kazakhstan dates to prehistoric times. Early Kazakhstanis made carvings and drawings on stone walls. The images show deer and other animals, riders on horseback, priests, hunters, and other scenes of ancient life. Some of the pictures are thousands of years old.

The Scythians had many talented artists among their ranks. They loved to work in gold. Archaeologists have found gold earrings, pendants, buckles, and other ornaments from Scythian times.

Through the centuries, Kazakhstanis carried on the artistic traditions of their ancestors. They used animal hair and fur to make carpets, clothing, and coverings for their yurts. They made saddles from wood and leather. They used bronze to create lanterns and drinking vessels. But such items weren't just useful—they were also beautiful. People trimmed tools, weapons, and other household items with silver, gold, turquoise, and other precious stones. They covered carpets, walls, and clothing with decorative patterns showing the sun, stars, crescent moons, animals, flowers, and geometric shapes.

Timur, who ruled southern Kazakhstan in the late 1300s, was a great patron of the arts. He oversaw the building of grand mosques and mausoleums throughout his territory. These structures featured dramatic domes, soaring arched entryways, and intricate and brilliantly colored tile work. The Ahmed Yassavi Mausoleum in the town of Turkistan is a fine example of architecture from the Timurid era.

The Russians added their own artistic touches when they arrived in Kazakhstan in the 1700s. They constructed ornate homes and public buildings with intricate brick and woodwork. They built massive churches topped by brilliant crosses and onion-shaped domes.

Artistic freedom came to a halt during the Soviet era. By government decree, all works had to be made in the Socialist realist style. That is, paintings and sculptures had to show farmers and workers toiling hard to build the perfect Communist society. The government filled cities throughout Kazakhstan with statues of Communist heroes such as Karl Marx and Vladimir Lenin. It constructed block after block of bland concrete apartment buildings to house workers.

With the fall of the Soviet Union, artistic freedom flourished once again in Kazakhstan. In the new capital of Astana, architects have set to work creating government buildings, museums, and other structures. Many of these places have a futuristic feel. For instance, the Alatau Sports Palace looks like a streamlined machine. Other buildings, such as the presidential headquarters with its green dome and spires, are reminiscent of traditional Islamic architecture.

Modern painters in Kazakhstan work in a variety of styles. Some make realistic scenes of people and the landscape. Others make abstract works. Many artists combine modern techniques and ideas with traditional Kazakhstani designs. Acclaimed Kazakhstani artists include painter Aimagul Menlibayeva and sculptor B. Norbekov.

Music and Dance

Music has always played a large role in Kazakhstani culture. Since ancient times, religious ceremonies, weddings, and other special events have included songs and dances. Ancient poets and storytellers often told their tales in song form, with instrumental accompaniment. Musicians played instruments such as clay whistles, reed flutes, and goatskin bagpipes. They played stringed instruments such as the *dombra* (similar to a lute) and the *kobyz* (similar to a violin).

Through the generations, Kazakhstani nomads maintained their musical traditions. They did not write down song lyrics or musical

Dombras, such as the ones played by these two girls, are popular throughout central Asia. To learn more about dombras and to hear what they sound like, visit www.vgsbooks.com for links.

Many Kazakhstanis learn traditional **Russian ballet,** which is more structured and formal than traditional Kazakh dances.

notes. They passed on tunes and songs by playing, singing, listening, and teaching one another. They learned dances the same way.

The influx of Russians from the 1700s through the 1900s brought new musical trends to Kazakhstan. Unlike Kazakhstan with its entirely folk tradition, Russia had a more classical musical heritage. The Russians created symphonies and operas with written scores. Russian ballets were carefully choreographed (planned out step-by-step).

During the Soviet era, the government founded many institutions for the promotion of classical music in Kazakhstan. These included the Abai State Academic Theater of Opera and Ballet, founded in 1933, and the Kurmangazy National Conservatory, founded in 1944. Many world-class musicians emerged from Kazakhstan during this era.

In modern times, Kazakhstan is still a hotbed of classical musicians. For instance, Alan Buribayev is an internationally acclaimed Kazakhstani conductor. Maria Muhamedkyzy is a leading opera singer. Aiman Musakojaeva is a famous violinist.

Folk music still thrives in Kazakhstan too. Many modern groups keep the old traditions alive. They play traditional instruments, wear authentic folk costumes, and sing the songs of their ancestors. Almaty's Philharmonic Central Concert Hall is a great place to hear folk music. Kazakhstan has a small rock/pop music scene. In big cities, young people like to visit nightclubs and listen to live bands, many of them from Russia.

Food

Kazakhstanis enjoy a variety of foods, many of which seem strange to foreign visitors. For instance, Kazakhstanis like dishes made with horse meat. *Kazy, karta,* and *chuchuk* are different kinds of horse meat sausage. Kazakhstanis also eat mutton (the meat of sheep), beef, goat meat, fish, and chicken. The national dish of Kazakhstan is *besbarmak*, made with onions, boiled beef, mutton, and sometimes horse meat, served over large flat noodles. Shashlik, or kebab, is another popular dish. It consists of cubes of meat grilled with vegetables.

Along with meats, Kazakhstanis eat a lot of rice and heavy noodles (called *laghman*). Dumplings (balls of meat wrapped in dough and then boiled, steamed, or fried) are popular. *Plov* is a favorite dish made with rice, meat, onions, carrots, and fruits such as apricots, raisins, and prunes. For a snack, people like to eat *baursaki*, which are fried balls of dough— a lot like doughnuts. They also love apples, which originated and grow in abundance around Almaty.

Kazakhstanis enjoy some unusual drinks, such as *kumys* (fermented mare's milk) and *shubat* (fermented camel's milk). They also like to

KAZAKHSTANI RICE

This Kazakhstani dish is tasty and easy to make.

1 pound finely ground lamb or ground beef

⅓ cup slivered almonds

½ cup chopped pitted dates

⅓ cup chopped pitted prunes

3 dried apricots, chopped

1 medium onion, chopped

1 tablespoon salt

2 cloves garlic, minced

1½ cups rice

1 tablespoon vegetable oil

1. In a large skillet over medium-high heat, cook the ground lamb or beef until browned and cooked through, stirring frequently and breaking up any large clumps.
2. Combine the meat, almonds, fruit, onion, salt, and garlic in a large bowl.
3. In a large saucepan, cook the rice according to the directions on the package until it is almost done—but do not drain it. Add the oil to the rice as it cooks.
4. Add the meat mixture to the rice and allow it to finish cooking.
5. Serve as a side dish or main course.

Serves 6

The **Zelyony Bazaar in Almaty** is known throughout central Asia. Vendors sell meat, nuts, and dried fruit, as shown above, and traditional foods such as fermented camel's milk.

drink tea, called *shay* in Kazakh. They use the milk of sheep, camels, goats, and cows to make a variety of cheeses, butter, and yogurt.

Holidays

Kazakhstanis observe eight national holidays. Like people in Western countries, they celebrate New Year's Day on January 1. March 8 is International Women's Day—a day on which men honor women, especially by doing household chores. March 22 is Navrus, a festival of spring. May 1 is called Unity of the Kazakhstani People Day—which honors the fellowship of Kazakhstan's different ethnic groups. May 9 is Victory Day, which commemorates the Allied victory in World War II. August 30 is Constitution Day, held to honor the creation of the nation's constitution in 1995. October 25 is the Day of Republic, which marks Kazakhstan's decision to declare its independence in 1991. December 16 is Independence Day—the day on which independence began in 1991.

Kazakhstanis also observe several religious holidays, depending on their faith. Muslims observe Ramadan, the ninth month of the Islamic calendar. During this month, Muslims take no food or drink from sunup to sundown. Evenings are devoted to prayer. At the end of the month, people hold a big feast called Eid al-Fitr. Members of the Russian Orthodox Church observe Christian holidays, including Easter and Christmas.

Sports

Kazakhstanis were the first people to tame and train horses. So it's no surprise that horseback riding is still a favorite pastime in Kazakhstan. In the game of *buzkashi*, two teams of horseback riders compete to carry the body of a dead sheep downfield. Other contests involve two riders trying to pull one another out of the saddle, riders trying to pick up a piece of cord or a coin from the ground while galloping on horseback at full speed, or long-distance horse races.

"NEW DAYS"

Navrus is the most festive holiday in Kazakhstan. The name means "new days," and the holiday marks the beginning of spring. People celebrate with a lot of food, horse racing, games, traditional costumes, folk music and dance, and parties. They also set up yurts in towns and cities. Navrus is not unique to Kazakhstan. People throughout central Asia celebrate the holiday.

Two men play **buzkashi.** The dead sheep hangs between the two horses.

An Ancient Art

Berkutchi, or hunting with eagles, is an ancient tradition in Kazakhstan. The tradition continues in modern times. Hunters *(above)* on the steppes train eagles or falcons to sight and capture prey, such as rabbits, foxes, and smaller birds.

Since Kazakhstan has a long, snowy winter, it's also no surprise that winter sports are popular. The Shimbulak ski resort outside Almaty has great downhill slopes. World-class ice-skaters train at the open-air Medeo speed skating rink, also outside Almaty. The Medeo speed skating rink is twice as big as a football field. Its surrounding stadium can seat up to twelve thousand spectators. Many world records have been set at the rink. Vladimir Smirnov, a cross-country skier, has won four Olympic medals for Kazakhstan, including a gold medal at the 1994 Winter Games in Lillehammer, Norway.

Visit www.vgsbooks.com for links to websites with additional information about the Medeo speed skating rink and what Medeo is like today. Also find information on Kazakhstan's Olympic medalists.

Kazakhstani athlete Alexander Vinokourov, a professional cyclist, won a silver medal at the 2000 Olympics and placed third at the 2003 Tour de France. Kazakhstan has also produced Olympic champions in track and field, boxing, wrestling, and weight lifting. Bakhtiyar Artayev, a welterweight boxer, won a gold medal at the 2004 Summer Olympics in Athens, Greece. Kazakhstanis also enjoy team sports such as ice hockey and soccer.

THE ECONOMY

Beginning in ancient times, the people of Kazakhstan made a living by raising animals. They traveled across the steppes with herds of sheep, goats, cattle, and horses. The animals provided people with meat, milk, skins, and transportation. People used wood and woolen cloth to build yurts. They made clothing from animal skins and furs. They made tools from wood, metal, and animal bones. Everything they needed to survive came from the land.

During the Soviet era, Kazakhstan became an industrialized nation. The government opened factories and mines throughout Kazakhstan. It forced people to settle down in cities or large farms. The nomadic life came to an end.

But the planned Soviet economy was not successful. Government-controlled farms and businesses could not provide enough goods to meet people's needs. Throughout the Soviet Union, people faced severe shortages of food and other consumer products. Most people lived poorly, in cramped, run-down apartments shared with other fam-

ilies. Cars were a luxury reserved for only the very rich. People's unhappiness with the economy, in part, led to the breakup of the Soviet Union in 1991.

A New System

With independence, Kazakhstanis were free to create a different kind of economy. Instead of Communism, they set up a capitalist system, like the system used in the United States and Western Europe. The system is based on private business ownership and free enterprise, with little government interference in business operations. After a shaky start, the new Kazakhstani economy grew quickly. Foreign companies arrived to do business in Kazakhstan. Foreign energy companies were especially eager to invest in Kazakhstan's rich fields of oil, natural gas, and minerals.

By the early 2000s, the Kazakhstani economy was strong, with a steady rate of growth. International lenders and foreign governments noted that the economy was well managed, with laws and regulations that encouraged business investment. The gross domestic product (GDP—the total value of goods and services produced in the country in one year) stood at $118.4 billion in 2004. Service work, including jobs in banking, communications, sales, tourism, insurance, and health care, accounted for 54.8 percent of the GDP. Industry, including mining, energy, and manufacturing work, made up 37.8 percent of the GDP, while agricultural work accounted for just 7.4 percent of the GDP.

The Rich Grow Richer

A small group of Kazakhstanis—mostly business and political leaders—grew rich after independence. They did so by investing in the oil business and other industries. In some cases, politicians took illegal payments from foreign energy companies.

But the wealth that a few Kazakhstanis enjoy has not trickled down to ordinary people. According to some reports, 19 percent of the population lives below the poverty level, and 8 percent of eligible workers are unemployed. But other sources say these figures are much higher. Poverty is particularly severe in farm areas and small towns. Since independence, thousands of rural Kazakhstanis have flocked to big cities, looking for work.

Kazakhstani oil workers lay an oil pipeline north of Qyzylorda. Oil is a great natural resource in Kazakhstan, but only a small group has benefited.

Two men work at the Shymkent **phosphorus plant.** Phosphorus, one of Kazakhstan's many natural resources, is used to make fertilizers.

Energy and Mining

Kazakhstan's economic strength rests on its vast stores of oil, natural gas, and minerals. According to some estimates, Kazakhstan might have oil reserves equaling 60 billion barrels. If this figure proves true, Kazakhstan is third in the world in oil wealth, behind only Saudi Arabia and Iraq. The largest oil stores are in the Kashagan field, beneath the Caspian Sea, and the Tengiz field, at the sea's northeastern edge. Working with Kazakhstan's government, multinational oil companies, including Chevron, Texaco, and BP (British Petroleum), have built facilities to extract, process, and transport Kazakhstani oil. These facilities include an extensive network of oil pipelines.

Kazakhstan also has vast supplies of natural gas, another valuable energy resource. Most gas fields are also located near or beneath the Caspian Sea. Coal is found in great abundance, especially around Qaraghandy and Ekibastuz in northeastern Kazakhstan. At other places, miners extract gold, silver, lead, zinc, iron, copper, chromium, manganese, bauxite, molybdenum, titanium, uranium, and other valuable minerals.

Other Industry

Kazakhstan's big cities, including Almaty, Semey, and Qaraghandy, are major industrial centers. Some factories produce fertilizers, chemicals, farm machinery, electric motors, construction materials, or clothing. Some process raw iron, copper, aluminum, and other minerals, while others process butter, cheese, yogurt, and other food products.

Agriculture

Kazakhstan has a rich agricultural history. At one time, nearly all the nation's people made a living by raising livestock and growing crops. In modern times, agriculture plays a much smaller role in the nation's economy, but farms are still important.

The most important farm crops are wheat, barley, rice, and cotton. Farmers also raise sheep, cattle, and other animals, which yield dairy products, leather, meat, and wool.

Fishing was once an enormous industry in Kazakhstan, with vast stocks of fish taken from the Caspian and Aral seas, as well as Lake Balkhash. With water pollution and the destruction of the Aral Sea, Kazakhstan's fishing industry has declined dramatically. The Caspian sturgeon, prized for its caviar, has dwindled in numbers. Fish processing plants have closed. In the 2000s, fishing no longer plays a significant role in Kazakhstan's agricultural economy.

Herders tend sheep in the northern part of Kazakhstan. At one time, most Kazakstanis worked as herders. In modern times, very few Kazakhstanis make a living herding animals.

Visit www.vgsbooks.com for links to websites with additional information about industry and agriculture in Kazakhstan. See the import and export figures, and find out the exchange rate from Kazakhstani tenge to U.S. dollars.

Imports and Exports

In 2004 Kazakhstan exported more than $18 billion in goods, while its imports totaled about $13 billion. Oil and natural gas are the nation's major export items, accounting for about 65 percent of all exports in 2004. Metals are another important item, making up nearly 20 percent of all exports in 2004. Other important export products are chemicals, machinery, grain, wool, meat, and coal. Kazakhstan's major export partners are Russia, Bermuda, Germany, China, France, and Italy.

Kazakhstan imports machinery and other equipment, chemicals, metal products, and food. Its main import partners are Russia, China, Germany, France, and Ukraine.

Tourists enjoy the slopes at a **ski resort in the Tian Mountains** near Almaty.

Tourism

During the Soviet era, Kazakhstan was off-limits to most foreign visitors. With independence, however, foreigners are free to visit Kazakhstan. There is much for a tourist to enjoy there: snowcapped mountains, dramatic rock formations, ski resorts, sparkling lakes, and fascinating history. The nation's tourism industry is small, but it is growing. To attract tourists, Kazakhstan has improved its roads, airline service, and hotels.

Transportation

Kazakhstan's biggest airports are found in Almaty and Astana, with air service to and from Moscow, Russia; Frankfurt, Germany; London, England; and other foreign cities. Air Astana is the nation's major airline.

When traveling within Kazakhstan, travelers can choose among airplanes, passenger trains, buses, and private cars. In the early 2000s, about 1.2 million Kazakhstanis owned cars. The nation has 8,500 miles (13,700 km) of railroad track and 51,000 miles (82,000 km) of

Many people in Kazakhstan travel from city to city by airplane. **Air Astana** is the official airline of Kazakhstan.

roads, 94 percent of which are paved. But winters are fierce in Kazakhstan—heavy snows can make traveling by car, train, or bus slow, dangerous, and sometimes impossible. As a result, many people choose to travel from city to city by air.

◉ Communications

Newspapers, radio and TV stations, and websites all offer news and information (in both Russian and Kazakh) to the people of Kazakhstan. Satellite and cable television give people access to international broadcasts. Computer use is growing, and Internet cafés are found in every big city. Kazakhstan also has a small film industry.

The Kazakhstani constitution guarantees freedom of the press and freedom of speech. But in reality, those freedoms are limited. Government regulations make it difficult and expensive for independent media to operate in Kazakhstan. President Nazarbayev has arrested journalists and shut down newspapers and websites that have criticized his administration. The Kazakhstani government owns several newspapers, television stations, and radio stations. This state-owned media always puts a pro-government spin on the news.

SORRY, WRONG NUMBER

Kazakhstan's phone service is out of date and unreliable. As in other countries, many people communicate with one another using cell phones.

The Darker Side

Kazakhstan's economy is not without troubles. Drug traffickers operate in Kazakhstan, shipping marijuana and other illegal drugs between central Asia and Europe. Other criminals deal in illegal weapons and prostitution. The Russian Mafia—an organized crime group—operates in all the former Soviet republics, including Kazakhstan. Violent crime has risen sharply since independence.

The oil business, which brings billions of dollars flowing into Kazakhstan, has been caught up in corruption. In a scandal known as Kazakhgate (named for the 1970s Watergate political scandal in the United States), top Kazakhstani officials were charged with taking bribes from Western oil companies in exchange for big government contracts. President Nazarbayev and his family members have also been charged with bribery, corruption, and wrongdoing.

The Future

What does the future hold for Kazakhstan? Most observers think its future looks bright. The nation's economy is growing, thanks mostly to the booming energy industry. In 2006, Kazakhstan launched its first communications satellite, a first step toward joining the small number of countries with their own space programs. It has an educated workforce, a rich cultural scene, and valuable natural resources. Kazakhstan is a peaceful nation and is not home to extremist movements. It faces serious environmental problems, but it is also working hard on environmental cleanup and restoration.

Kazakhstan occupies an important spot on the world stage. It sits between Russia and China, two of the most powerful nations in the world, and has good relations with both nations. It also has friendly relations with the United States and the countries of Europe. It has vast stores of oil and other energy resources, which make many nations eager to do business there. As the economy has grown, a

THE EXTREMIST THREAT

Many parts of the Middle East and central Asia are home to Islamist extremists—people who want their government and society to run according to strict Islamic law. Some Islamist extremists have links to terrorist groups. Although Kazakhstan has a large Islamic population, it has few Islamist extremists. But this situation might change as Islamist extremism spreads throughout the world. The Kazahkstani government is wary of Islamist extremism. Government security forces work hard to keep foreign Islamists from organizing inside Kazakhstan.

small group of Kazakhstanis have grown rich. But many more Kazakhstanis remain poor.

When Kazakhstan first became independent, it operated as a democracy. But in the early 2000s, democracy hangs in the balance in Kazakhstan. President Nazarbayev attacks those who criticize him, including journalists and political opponents. He has changed the nation's constitution, manipulated elections, and tightened his grip over every branch of government. Many charge that Nazarbayev has abandoned democratic principles in favor of dictatorship.

Kazakhstanis hope that their nation's economic success will continue. They also hope this new success will benefit all citizens—not just a small group of business and political leaders. Most of all, Kazakhstanis want a true democracy and true democratic rights and freedoms.

CA. 13,000 B.C.	Prehistoric peoples live in Kazakhstan.
CA. 8000 B.C.	Ancient Kazakhstanis learn to tame, train, and ride horses.
600s B.C.	Scythian culture emerges in Kazakhstan.
100s B.C.	The Usuns, a people from Mongolia, invade Kazakhstan.
A.D. 400s	Asian warriors called Huns invade Kazakhstan.
500s	Turkic peoples invade Kazakhstan from Mongolia.
900s	The Karakhanid Turks take over Kazakhstan. The Islamic religion starts to spread through Kazakhstan.
1130	Khitans invade Kazakhstan from northern China.
1220s	The Mongol warrior Genghis Khan conquers central Asia.
1258	Berke Khan establishes Islam as the official religion of the Golden Horde (western and northern Kazakhstan).
1370s	Timur begins to build an empire in central Asia.
1400s	Central Asia breaks into khanates, territories ruled by local khans.
1500s	People called Kazakhs break away from the Uzbek Khanate. They create three new groupings: the Great Horde, Middle Horde, and Little Horde.
1600s-1700s	Jungars from China make raids into Kazakh territory.
EARLY 1700s	The Kazakh hordes ask Russia for protection from the Jungars.
1720s	Russian soldiers begin arriving in Kazakhstan.
LATE 1700s	Russian settlers start to take over Kazakhstani land.
1800s	Russia tightens its control over Kazakhstan. Kazakhs unsuccessfully revolt against Russian rule.
1914	Russia enters World War I.
1916	Kazakh fighters revolt against Russian control, again unsuccessfully.
1917	Bolsheviks seize control of the Russian government.
1918-1920	Kazakhstan's Alash Orda Party sides with the White Army to fight the Communist Red Army.
1922	Communist leaders create the Union of Soviet Socialist Republics.
1929	Alma-Ata becomes the capital of Soviet Kazakhstan. Joseph Stalin comes to power in the Soviet Union.

1930s The Soviet government forces Kazakhstanis to abandon their nomadic lifestyle.

1939 World War II begins in Europe.

1941 Germany attacks the Soviet Union. Joseph Stalin sends ethnic Soviets to live in Kazakhstan and other central Asian republics.

1949 The Soviet Union begins testing nuclear weapons in Kazakhstan.

1955 The Soviet Union builds the Baikonur Cosmodrome, a space center in Kazakhstan.

1958 Nikita Khrushchev creates the Virgin Lands Campaign, a plan to farm the Kazakhstani steppes.

1962 Aleksandr Solzhenitsyn publishes *One Day in the Life of Ivan Denisovich*, based on his experiences in a Kazakhstani gulag.

1969 Archaeologists find the grave of the Golden Man, a Scythian warrior.

1960s AND 1970s Soviet citizens face shortages of food and other consumer goods.

1985 Mikhail Gorbachev becomes leader of the Soviet Union. He announces a series of political reforms, including glasnost and perestroika.

1986 Gennady Kolbin, a Russian, becomes head of the Communist Party of Kazakhstan. His appointment leads to violent protests in Alma-Ata.

1989 Mikhail Gorbachev appoints Nursultan Nazarbayev, a Kazakh, to lead the Communist Party in Kazakhstan.

1991 Communist leaders attempt to seize power from Gorbachev. The Soviet Union breaks apart. Kazakhstan becomes an independent nation on December 16.

1992 Kazakhstan joins the United Nations.

1993 Alma-Ata changes its name to Almaty.

1997 Astana becomes Kazakhstan's new capital city.

2001 Kazakhstan offers support to the United States in its war against terrorism.

2003 Kazakhstan sends troops to assist the U.S.-led coalition in the Iraq war.

2005 Nursultan Nazarbayev is reelected president with more than 90 percent of the vote. International observers charge that the election is unfair.

2006 Kazakhstan adopts a new national anthem, "Mening Qazaqstanym" or "My Kazakhstan." Kazakhstan launches its first communications satellite.

COUNTRY NAME: Republic of Kazakhstan

AREA: 1,048,300 square miles (2,715,097 sq. km)

MAIN LANDFORMS: Altay Mountains, Betpaqdala Desert, Caspian Depression, Chu-Ily Mountains, Greater Barsuki Desert, Qaratau Range, Kyzyl Kum Desert, Moyynqum Desert, Tian Mountains, Ustyurt Plateau

HIGHEST POINT: Mount Khan Tengri (20,990 feet, or 6,398 m)

LOWEST POINT: Vpadina Kaundy (433 feet, or 132 m, below sea level)

MAJOR RIVERS: Ertis, Esil, Ile, Syr, Tobyl, Ural, Zhem

ANIMALS: antelope, Bactrian camels, bears, caracals, Caspian seals, eagles, elk, falcons, foxes, gazelles, snow leopards, sturgeon, wild sheep, wolves

CAPITAL CITY: Astana

OTHER MAJOR CITIES: Almaty, Atyrau, Qaraghandy, Taraz

OFFICIAL LANGUAGES: Kazakh, Russian

MONETARY UNIT: tenge. 1 tenge = 100 tiyn.

KAZAKHSTANI CURRENCY

In the first years of independence, Kazakhstan used Russian currency, based on a unit of money called the ruble. In 1993 Kazakhstan created its own currency, based on a unit called the tenge. Tenge is a Kazakh word meaning "balance" or "scales."

The tenge is divided into 100 tiyn. The Kazakhstani government issues banknotes (paper money) worth 3, 5, 10, 20, 50, 100, 200, 500, 1,000, 2,000, 5,000, and 10,000 tenge. It issues coins worth 1, 3, 5, 10, 20, and 50 tiyn. In early 2006, it took 128 tenge to equal one U.S. dollar.

Kazakhstani banknotes feature pictures of famous buildings, mountains, riders on horseback, and other scenes from Kazakhstani life. They also show portraits of famous people. Most notes carry a picture of al-Farabi, a great scientist and philosopher born in Kazakhstan in the A.D. 870s.

The Kazakhstani flag is a field of light blue, which stands for Kazakhstan's blue skies. The center shows a yellow sun, representing prosperity, and a soaring eagle, which symbolizes Kazakhstan's flight toward greatness. On the left is a decorative yellow band, representing the nation's rich cultural heritage. The flag was designed by Shaken Niyazbekov. It was adopted on June 4, 1992.

Kazakhstan's national anthem is "Mening Qazaqstanym" or "My Kazakhstan," a patriotic song written in 1958. Zhumeken Nazhimedenov wrote the original lyrics, but President Nursultan Nazarbayev made some changes to the words in the early 2000s. Shamshi Kaldayakov composed the music. Kazakhstan adopted the song as its national anthem in 2006. It is normally sung in either Kazakh or Russian. Here are the English lyrics:

Golden sun in heaven,
Golden corn in steppe,
Legend of courage—
It is my land.
In oldest antiquity
Our glory was born,
Proud and strong
Are my Kazakh people.

I've a boundless expanse
And a way, opened in future.
I have an independent,
United people.
Like an ancient friend
Our happy land,
Our happy people
Are welcoming new time.

CHORUS
My country, my country,
As your flower I'll grow,
As your song I'll stream, country!
My native land—Kazakhstan!

For a link where you can listen to the Kazakhstani national anthem, go to www.vgsbooks.com.

BAKHTIYAR ARTAYEV (b. 1983) Born in Taraz, boxer Bakhtiyar Artayev is a seven-time Kazakhstani national champion. At the 2004 Summer Olympic Games in Athens, Greece, he defeated powerful Cuban boxer Lorenzo Aragon Armenteros to win a gold medal. Weighing about 152 pounds (69 kg), Artayev competed in the welterweight category. After his gold-medal performance, he returned to a fabulous victory celebration in Taraz.

ALTYNAI ASYLMURATOVA (b. 1961) Asylmuratova is an acclaimed ballerina, born in Alma-Ata (modern-day Almaty). As a young woman, she studied dance at the Vaganova Ballet Academy in Leningrad (modern-day Saint Petersburg), Russia. She went on to perform with Russian ballet companies. She has toured extensively in the West, appearing with the American Ballet Theatre, the British Royal Ballet, the Paris Opera Ballet, and other companies. In 2000 she became artistic director of the Vaganova Academy.

TOKTAR AUBAKIROV (b. 1946) Aubakirov was Kazakhstan's first cosmonaut (Soviet astronaut). Born near Qaraghandy, he joined the Soviet air force, where he worked as a parachutist and a test pilot. In 1991 he entered the Soviet space program as a research cosmonaut. He flew into space for almost eight days as a member of the *Soyuz TM-13* mission in 1991. In 1993 he became director of the National Aerospace Agency in Kazakhstan. He later served in Kazakhstan's legislature.

ALAN BURIBAYEV (b. 1979) Born into a family of musicians in Almaty, Buribayev studied violin and conducting at Kazakh National Conservatory. He continued his studies at the University of Music in Vienna. After graduation, Buribayev served as a guest conductor with symphonies around the world, including the London Philharmonic Orchestra, the Danish National Symphony Orchestra, the Baltimore Symphony Orchestra, and the Hungarian National Philharmonic Orchestra. He is also the principal conductor of the Astana Symphony Orchestra in Kazakhstan.

AL-FARABI (c. 878–950) Although his precise birthplace is unknown, some scholars think al-Farabi was born near modern-day Otrar in Kazakhstan. As an adult, al-Farabi lived in Baghdad in modern-day Iraq. There he studied mathematics, philosophy, medicine, and music. He wrote several books, including a commentary on the work of the great Greek philosopher Aristotle. Al-Farabi's teachings influenced many later philosophers. His portrait appears on Kazakhstani banknotes.

ABAI KUNANBAEV (1845–1904) Abai Kunanbaev is considered Kazakhstan's first great poet. He was born in Kaskabulak in eastern Kazakhstan. As a boy, he studied Russian language and literature, as well as Islamic teachings. He was one of the first Kazakhstani poets to put his works into written form. He also translated foreign works into Kazakh. His poems examine Eastern and Western culture, as well as nature and politics. In addition to writing poetry, Abai also composed music and studied philosophy.

AIMAGUL MENLIBAYEVA (b. 1969) Menlibayeva is a visual artist who creates paintings, photographs, films, and multimedia installations. Her work often draws on religious concepts, including themes found in Sufism and Buddhism. She has shown her work in Kazakhstan and in international art exhibits such as the Venice Biennial and the Sydney Biennial. Menlibayeva was born in Alma-Ata.

DAREZHAN OMIRBAYEV (b. 1958) Filmmaker Omirbayev was born in Oyyq. In 1980 he enrolled in Kazakh State University, where he studied mathematics. After graduation, he enrolled at the VGIK film school in Moscow, Russia. There, he studied film history and theory. From 1987 to 1989, Omirbayev edited a Russian journal called *New Film*. He has directed several fictional and documentary films of his own. His film *Killer* won a prize at the 1998 Cannes Film Festival in France.

ALTYNBEK SARSENBAEV (1962–2006) Born in the village of Qaynar near Almaty, Sarsenbaev was a leading figure in Kazakhstani politics. He served in top government positions, including mayor of Almaty, information minister with the national government, and ambassador to Russia. In 2003 Sarsenbaev broke with the Nazarbayev administration, which he saw as dictatorial and corrupt. He formed the True Bright Path Party, hoping to run for president in late 2005. But shortly after announcing his candidacy, Sarsenbaev was beaten and then murdered. Although others have been charged in the murder, observers believe that President Nazarbayev had Sarsenbaev killed to silence him.

OLGA SHISHIGINA (b. 1968) In the 1990s and early 2000s, Shishigina was a top competitor in the women's 100- and 60-meter hurdles. She won championships throughout Asia and won a gold medal at the Summer Olympic Games in Sydney, Australia, in 2000. Shishigina was born in Almaty. Due to injuries, she retired from track and field in the early 2000s.

AHMED YASSAVI MAUSOLEUM Yassavi was a twelfth-century holy man who lived most of his life in the Kazakhstani town of Turkistan. When he died, his followers built him a small mausoleum (tomb). In the 1390s, the emperor Timur ordered construction of a much grander tomb for Yassavi. The impressive sight in Turkistan features intricate tile work, towering archways, and ornately carved doorways.

MEDEO ICE RINK Located in the hills outside Almaty, this open-air skating rink measures 113,000 square feet (10,500 sq. m)—twice as big as a football field. The rink was built in 1972 to train speed skaters. Many champion Soviet skaters have trained here. The rink is open to the public on weekends.

MOUNT KHAN TENGRI To those who practice the ancient religion of Tengrism, this peak is sacred—the meeting place of heaven and earth. The peak also attracts high-altitude mountain climbers. The top portion of the mountain is made of marble, which glows red at sunrise and sunset.

PRESIDENT'S MUSEUM OF KAZAKHSTAN Located in the capital of Astana, this museum tells the history of Kazakhstan, from the Stone Age to the Space Age. The most fascinating exhibit is a replica of the Scythian-era Golden Man costume. (The real costume is kept inside vaults at Kazakhstan's national bank.)

SAINT NICOLAS CATHEDRAL Built in 1909, this cathedral in Almaty offers visitors a taste of czarist Russia. The cathedral has gold onion domes on top, vivid icons (religious images) inside, and a lot of dramatic candlelight. The cathedral was used as a military horse stable during the Russian Revolution.

SHARYN CANYON This dramatic canyon east of Almaty features strange and colorful rock formations. The Sharyn River, flowing down from the Tian Mountains, has carved out the canyon over thousands of years.

SINGING SAND DUNE Located in the Altyn-Emel National Park, this dune makes a low humming noise when the wind blows. The surrounding park is home to antelope, camels, and golden eagles.

TAMGALY-TAS PETROGLYPHS This site near Lake Balkash contains a thousand or more petroglyphs (rock drawings) created by early Kazakhstanis. Some drawings show prehistoric hunters and deer. Other, later pictures depict the Buddha, the founder of the Buddhist religion.

capitalism: an economic system based on private property and free enterprise, with little government interference in business operations

Cold War: a time of hostility between the United States and the Soviet Union that lasted from 1945 until 1991

collective: a large government-run farm

Communism: an economic system in which the central government controls all business activity, including employment, management, manufacturing, pricing, and sales

corruption: widespread dishonesty, bribery, and other illegal activity

czar: the title given to Russian emperors between 1547 and 1917

democracy: a form of government in which citizens vote for their own leaders. Most democratic governments guarantee people freedom of speech, freedom of religion, and other basic rights.

fertilizers: chemicals used to boost plant growth

glasnost: a Soviet policy, enacted in 1986, that gave people more freedom of speech. The word *glasnost* means "openness" in Russian.

gulag: a Soviet-era prison camp

irrigation: a system of channels, pumps, and other devices used to carry water to crops

Islam: a religion founded by the prophet Muhammad in the A.D. 600s. Islam is widespread in central Asia and around the world.

Kazakh: a descendant of the early nomadic inhabitants of Kazakhstan; the language of Kazakhstan

Muslim: a member of the Islamic faith

nomad: a person who travels from place to place, according to the season, with herds of livestock

nuclear fallout: radioactive particles spread through the air after the explosion of nuclear bombs

Oralman: a Kazakh living outside Kazakhstan

perestroika: a Soviet policy, enacted in 1986, that loosened government control over business and politics. *Perestroika* means "restructuring" in Russian.

pesticides: chemicals used to kill insects on crops

Russian Orthodox Church: a branch of the Christian Church based in Russia

Scythians: an ancient civilization that originated in Kazakhstan in the 600s B.C.

steppes: vast, treeless plains covered by grasses

trafficker: someone who carries on illegal buying and selling

yurt: a portable tent, made of wood and felt and traditionally used by central Asian nomads

Glossary

"Background Note: Kazakhstan." *U.S. Department of State, Bureau of South and Central Asian Affairs.* **2006.**
http://www.state.gov/r/pa/ei/bgn/5487.htm **(March 2006).**
This U.S. State Department site provides a host of statistics on Kazakhstan, its people, its government, and its economy.

"Country Profile: Kazakhstan." *BBC News.* **2005.**
http://news.bbc.co.uk/1/hi/world/asia-pacific/country_profiles/1298071.stm **(March 2006).**
This site provides an overview of Kazakhstani society, with links to in-depth articles on current events.

"A Country Study: Kazakhstan." *Federal Research Division, Library of Congress.* **2005.**
http://memory.loc.gov/frd/cs/kztoc.html **(March 2006).**
This site examines Kazakhstan in depth, including geography, history, society, and government.

Fergus, Michael, and Janar Jandosova. *Kazakhstan: Coming of Age.* **London: Stacey International, 2003.**
This comprehensive title sheds light on Kazakhstan in the twenty-first century, from the nation's landscape and history to its artists and social scene. Lush photographs accompany the text.

Glazebrook, Philip. *Journey to Khiva: A Writer's Search for Central Asia.* **New York: Kodansha International, 1994.**
The author details his travels through the nations of central Asia. The travel narrative is interspersed with information on Kazakhstani history and culture.

Grousset, René. *The Empire of the Steppes: A History of Central Asia.* **Translated by Naomi Walford. New Brunswick, NJ: Rutgers University Press, 1970.**
Beginning with prehistory and ending with the Mongol invasion, the author traces central Asian history in great detail.

"Kazakhstan." *CIA World Factbook.* **2005.**
http://www.cia.gov/cia/publications/factbook/geos/kz.html **(March 2006).**
Compiled by the Central Intelligence Agency, this site offers up-to-date facts and statistics on Kazakhstan's geography, environment, population, government, and economy.

"Kazakhstan." *Population Reference Bureau.* **2005.**
http://www.prb.org/TemplateTop.cfm?Section=PRB_Country_Profiles&template=/customsource/countryprofile/countryprofiledisplay.cfm&Country=398 **(March 2006).**
This site offers country-by-country statistics on health, family planning, poverty, and other topics.

Kleveman, Lutz. *The New Great Game: Blood and Oil in Central Asia.* **New York: Grove Press, 2004.**
Central Asia—especially Kazakhstan—is rich in valuable oil and natural gas. Thus the United States, Russia, China, and other countries are all interested in control and influence in the region. This book examines the political complexities of this situation.

Selected Bibliography

Mayhew, Bradley, Paul Clammer, and Michael Kohn. *Central Asia.* **Footscray, Victoria, AUS: Lonely Planet Publications, 2004.**
This well-researched guidebook is written for visitors to Kazakhstan, Uzbekistan, Kyrgyzstan, Tajikistan, Afghanistan, and Turkmenistan. The book offers comprehensive information on each nation's history, culture, and people, with practical details for travelers.

Moorhouse, Geoffrey. *On the Other Side: A Journey Through Soviet Central Asia.* **New York: Henry Holt and Company, 1990.**
The author traveled through central Asia in 1989, right before the demise of the Soviet Union. His book paints a vivid and complex picture of central Asian politics, culture, and society.

Olcott, Martha Brill. *Central Asia's Second Chance.* **Washington, DC: Carnegie Endowment for International Peace, 2005.**
After the fall of the Soviet Union, many people were hopeful that democracy would flourish in central Asia. So far, that hope hasn't been realized. The author investigates the reasons.

———. *Kazakhstan: Unfulfilled Promise.* **Washington, DC: Carnegie Endowment for International Peace, 2002.**
Independent Kazakhstan has many problems, including a corrupt government, political repression, and a growing gulf between rich and poor. The author examines the young nation and its troubles.

Rashid, Ahmed. *Jihad: The Rise of Militant Islam in Central Asia.* **New York: Penguin Books, 2003.**
Radical Islam is on the rise in the nations of central Asia. The author examines the complexities of religion and politics in the region.

Roston, Keith. *Once in Kazakhstan: The Snow Leopard Emerges.* **New York: iUniverse, Inc., 2005.**
The author, an expert in Soviet and post-Soviet studies, offers personal insights into life and travel in independent Kazakhstan.

Roy, Olivier. *The New Central Asia: The Creation of Nations.* **New York: New York University Press, 2000.**
The author presents a thorough political analysis of the governments that have emerged in Kazakhstan, Turkmenistan, Uzbekistan, Tajikistan, Kyrgyzstan, and Azerbaijan after independence.

Thubron, Colin. *The Lost Heart of Asia.* **New York: Perennial, 1994.**
The author toured the five central Asian republics shortly after independence. His book offers insights into central Asian life and culture.

Cheneviere, Alain. *Central Asia: The Sons of Tamburlaine.* **Paris: Vilo International, 2001.**
This lush photography book offers images of the people, land, and society of central Asia.

Corrigan, Jim. *Kazakhstan.* **Broomall, PA: Mason Crest Publishers, 2005.**
This book is part of a series on the growth and influence of Islam in central Asia. Islam is a dominant religion in Kazakhstan, and Islamist extremism may be on the rise there. The author examines the situation in detail.

DK Publishing. *Islam.* **New York: DK Children, 2005.**
This beautifully illustrated book gives readers insight into Islam, a dominant religion in Kazakhstan.

Gottfried, Ted. *The Stalinist Empire.* **Minneapolis: Lerner Publications Company, 2002.**
Joseph Stalin imprisoned and murdered millions of Soviet citizens—including many Kazakhstanis—during his reign. This book sheds light on this brutal period in Soviet history.

Kort, Michael G. *The Handbook of the Former Soviet Union.* **Minneapolis: Lerner Publications Company, 1997.**
This comprehensive reference book looks at the former Soviet republics, including Kazakhstan, and examines their history and their futures.

Márquez, Herón. *Russia in Pictures.* **Minneapolis: Twenty-First Century Books, 2004.**
This book in the Visual Geography Series® introduces readers to Russia, a country with a profound influence on Kazakhstan. It tells about Russia's land, history, government, people, culture, and economics.

Pavlovic, Zoran. *Kazakhstan.* **New York: Chelsea House Publications, 2003.**
This title for young readers offers an overview of Kazakhstani history, geography, culture, and economics.

Ross, Stewart. *The Collapse of Communism.* **Chicago: Heinemann, 2004.**
This book for young readers examines the Communist philosophy and how Communism ultimately failed in the Soviet Union.

Tay, Alan. *Welcome to Kazakhstan.* **Milwaukee: Gareth Stevens Publishing, 2005.**
This title offers an introduction to Kazakhstan for young readers.

Traditional Culture and Folklore of Central Asia.
http://intangiblenet.freenet.uz/eng.htm
Visitors to this site can click on links to the nations of central Asia and learn about their traditional architecture, music, folklore, and more.

vgsbooks.com
http://www.vgsbooks.com
Visit vgsbooks.com, the home page of the Visual Geography Series®. You can get linked to all sorts of useful online information, including geographical, historical, demographic, cultural, and economic websites. The vgsbooks.com site is a great resource for late-breaking news and statistics.

"Welcome to the Embassy of Kazakhstan to the USA and Canada."
Embassy of Kazakhstan to the United States and Canada.
http://www.homestead.com/prosites-kazakhembus/
The website of Kazakhstan's embassy provides a host of information, from current events to business news to tourist information.

Whiting, Jim. *The Life and Times of Genghis Khan*. Hockessin, DE: Mitchell Lane Publishers, 2005.
Genghis Khan was fierce and bloodthirsty, but many Kazakhstanis consider him a hero. They look with pride at their famous ancestor, who created an enormous kingdom on the central Asian steppes. This book tells his story.

Zuehlke, Jeffrey. *Joseph Stalin*. Minneapolis: Lerner Publications Company, 2006.
The Stalinist era was a particularly bleak one for Kazakhstan and the other central Asian nations. This insightful biography examines the cruel dictator who brought terror and despair to the Soviet Union.

Captions for photos appearing on cover and chapter openers:

Cover: A Kazakhstani man practices the ancient art of berkutchi, hunting hares, foxes, and wolves with his golden eagle.

pp. 4–5 The Tian Mountains rise to the south and east of Almaty.

pp. 8–9 The sun sets over the steppes in Kazakhstan.

pp. 34–35 Children sit on a fence in Beyneu. Beyneu is located between the Caspian and Aral seas.

pp. 44–45 A Kazakhstani family celebrates the Islamic festival of Nauris, or New Year, inside a yurt.

pp. 56–57 Aqtau is the main seaport for Kazakhstan on the Caspian Sea. Many natural resources that Kazakhstan exports, such as metal, timber, and oil, are sent out through Aqtau.

Photo Acknowledgments
The images in this book are used with the permission of: © Igor Burganinov/Art Directors, pp. 4–5, 38, 49, 60–61; © XNR Productions, pp. 6, 11; Martin Barlow/Art Directors, pp. 8–9, 46, 52; © Vyacheslav Oseledko/AFP/Getty Images, pp. 12, 42; © Oleg Nikishin/Getty Images, pp. 13, 58; © Reuters/CORBIS, pp. 14, 54; © J. Palanca/SuperStock, p. 16; © Martin Moos/Lonely Planet Images, p. 17; © Shamil Zhumatov/Reuters/CORBIS, pp. 18–19; © SuperStock, Inc./SuperStock, p. 22; © David Samuel Robbins/CORBIS, p. 23; © AFP/Getty Images, p. 26; Dwight D. Eisenhower Library, p. 27; © Bettmann/CORBIS, p. 28; © Sergey Bondarenko/Kazakhstan Presidential Press Service/Reuters/CORBIS, p. 30; © Alexander Nemenov/AFP/Getty Images, p. 31; © Ahmad Al-Rubaye/AFP/Getty Images, p. 32; © Wolfgang Kaehler, 2006-www.wkaehlerphoto.com, pp. 34–35; © Trip/Art Directors, p. 36; © Robert Wallis/CORBIS, p. 39; © Liba Taylor/CORBIS, p. 41; © Paul Lowe/Panos Pictures, pp. 44–45; © Yuri Varigin/Art Directors, p. 50; © Paul Howell/Peter Arnold, Inc., p. 53; © A. Ustinenko/Peter Arnold, Inc., pp. 56–57; © Gerd Ludwig/Panos Pictures, p. 59; © Simon Richmond/Lonely Planet Images, p. 62; © Ignatiy Savaranskiy-www.aviaphoto.ru, p. 63; Audrius Tomonis-www.banknotes.com, p. 68; Laura Westlund/Independent Picture Service, p. 69.

Front Cover: © Jez Coulson/Insight/Panos Pictures
Back Cover: NASA